Dedication

To Buddie
Who teaches me daily the importance of story.

Contents

Teaching Early Writing -and- Reading Together

Mini-Lessons that Link K-2 Literacy Instruction

Connie Campbell Dierking

Teaching Early Writing and Reading Together:
Mini-lessons that Link K-2 Literacy Instruction
Connie Campbell Dierking

Book Design: Maria Messenger
Layout and Cover Design: Mickey Cuthbertson

Library of Congress Cataloging-in-Publication Data

Dierking, Connie Campbell, 1956-
  Teaching early writing and reading together : mini-lessons that link
K-2 literacy instruction / Connie Campbell Dierking.
      p. cm.
  Includes bibliographical references.
  ISBN-13: 978-1-625213-26-6 (pbk.)
  1. Language arts (Primary) 2. Reading (Primary) 3. English
language--Composition and exercises--Study and teaching (Primary) I.
Title.
LB1528.D54 2007
372.6--dc22
                              2007036791

Maupin House Publishing, Inc.
1710 Roe Crest Drive
North Mankato, MN 56003
888-262-6135
www.maupinhouse.com

Publishing Professional Resources that Improve Classroom Performance

Acknowledgments

I find myself blessed with the realization that my professional and personal "thank you" lists are as closely entwined as the braided gardenia outside my kitchen window. It took me awhile to discover that the best of friends also make the best of mentors. I know now that the long reach of literacy affects every part of your being, gathering all who stand with you into its embrace. For every teacher, administrator, supervisor, custodian, parent, and student who has shown me what it means to give and receive the gift of living literate, this hug is for you.

Thank you, first, to the educators of four special schools, Ready, Berringer, Wadsworth, and Lincoln Elementary in Griffith, Indiana. I continue to learn from these dedicated teachers who don't just "think I can" when it comes to building a curriculum of writing. Their work shouts, "I know I can!"

Deanna Texel, Jeani Fullard, Donna Rippley, and Gail Ramsdell, reading language arts and early childhood supervisors for Pinellas County schools: Thank you for your commitment to retaining writing workshop as a bottom line for every grade, every day.

To Mary Osborne, Holly Slaughter, and Christy Curran, the girls of the Writing Department of Pinellas County Schools, your expertise, passion, and heart for the teaching of writing will always be the words in my head.

A special thank you goes out to my reading coach buddies, who listened to my monthly rants about the reading and writing connection. Dawn, thanks for the many technology lessons.

To the teachers at Ponce De Leon Elementary, for your willingness to share your classrooms, your students, and their writing I will be eternally grateful. This book could not have been written without you.

Susan Palmer, thank you for being curious about the primary world and asking questions that always make me think.

Thank you Eyvonne Ryan, my newest partner in spreading the word: all children deserve extraordinary teachers. She is a living, breathing example.

To Cathy Torres, I am always in awe of your clarity of vision and earnestness of purpose as you take us all by the hand and lead us outside the box.

Sherra Jones, although the words of this book are mine, your influence is and will always be in every word that I share.

My family over the years has grown accustomed to my need for sharing the writing work of my students with others. I thank them again for their patience, large spaces of quiet time, and belief that this work—helping young writers find their voice—is worthy.

Introduction

> What is being learned in beginning reading overlaps with, and informs, what is being learned in beginning writing if it is allowed to do so… Learning to write contributes to the building of almost every new kind of inner control needed to become a successful reader…
>
> —Marie Clay

For as long as I have been an educator, I have heard about the reading/writing connection. Conversations in the teachers' lounge would include the suggestion of a reading/writing connection, the implication that everybody knows about a reading/writing connection, or a disbelief that anyone would ever suggest that reading and writing were not connected. We would all agree that writing and reading should not be separated, wipe the lunch from our faces, then race off to pick up our students from the lunchroom.

But acknowledging that there was a connection between reading and writing was unfortunately the extent of connecting reading and writing in our classrooms. Even teachers that I knew to be on top of their games did not seem to be able to verbalize exactly how they should teach the link between reading and writing to their students. Ultimately, I realized that I didn't really know, either.

So what **do** we really mean by "the reading/writing connection"? How does early writing instruction reinforce early reading instruction? How are the reading and writing processes alike and how were they different? What's the best way to teach students that the same processes they use when encoding information can be employed while decoding information?

This book will show primary teachers how to teach early writing and reading simultaneously, to intertwine instruction in the two processes of literacy. It is the result of my professional journey towards finding connections that I could hear, see, and explicitly teach.

I began by reflecting on my experience with teaching writing and examining what the reading/writing connection looked and sounded like in a classroom filled with budding readers and writers. In 2001 and 2002, Susan McElveen and I wrote books of explicit mini-lessons built around quality children's literature models. Our lessons targeted reading skills that could be introduced and then practiced during writer's workshop. We deliberately chose skills we knew were tested on most high stakes reading assessments—*cause and effect*, *sequencing*, and *comparing and contrasting*.

We were discouraged by the misunderstanding that the writing Target Skills® taught that very day in writer's workshop would not be explicitly reinforced by the teacher during reading instruction. The results were sometimes frustrating: Students who were writing with ellipses would read right through them during independent reading. Students using word-wall words to help them **write** words couldn't **read** those same words in small-group reading. Students who were taught to leave nice spaces between words during a writing conference had no one-to-one match during a reading conference.

I began to question my teacher friends: "How exactly are you connecting reading and writing in your classroom?" A few told me that they read trade books and then their students wrote innovations to go with the book. Others mentioned that their students would write alternate endings to stories shared in class or would write letters to favorite authors. Some teachers mentioned assigning reflections on books read for student journals.

While these do connect reading and writing, my vision for developing this incredibly important relationship was much deeper. I realized then that many teachers were thinking of the reading/writing connection only literally. They were having students write under the influence of literature the class had read, but that was the end of the connection. Students could mimic a structure or admire a word, but the idea of reminding them—during reading workshop—of a strategy introduced and practiced during writing workshop, was foreign. I really wanted students to develop a habit of mind: thinking like a reader **and** a writer at the same time.

I surmised that if my colleagues—all talented primary teachers—were not demonstrating the important connectors of literacy learning to their students, the writing/reading connection was probably not happening anywhere. Maybe teachers did not consider fully that the awareness of how a story goes is just as important in writing as it is in reading. Understanding that print is used to construct meaning, develop knowledge of letter names and sounds, and activate prior knowledge is just as foundational for successful writing as for successful reading. Perhaps it was time to bring the 'how' of connecting re-reading and writing to fruition.

The mini-lessons I share in this book were created to be taught first during writer's workshop. Since the guidelines of Reading First and many K-12 plans require a 90-minute uninterrupted block of time for the teaching of reading, it is difficult to include process writing in your reading block. However, teaching these Target Skills® during writer's workshop will provide students the strategies for purposeful reading during the reading block.

An example: One day during writer's workshop, my mini-lesson was to write with more specific words. One of my students was struggling with continually writing with boring words. The word in question on this day was *mad*. After a short conference around better words for *mad,* she changed the word *mad* to *furious.* We were both thrilled with the results. Later that day during independent reading, she stalled on the word *clever.* I was able to remind her of the work she had done during writing to choose a more specific word. We talked about the character in her book. He was not only smart but could read people very well. Using what she had learned about more specific words during writer's workshop she was able to make the connection and use the same strategy to read the word *clever.*

Each mini-lesson identifies the connecting point to reading. These Target Skills® can, and should, be revisited and reinforced during your reading block. And—truly!—these important skills and strategies could be practiced in any content area where it would seem natural. The use of a word wall should not come only during the reading block. Writing from left-to-right and top-to-bottom should happen every time a student composes a written response to reading. Students practice phonics through temporary spelling used in writing their own pieces. Student pieces can become a child's first written text and can become a jumping off point for reading. These simple published pieces should occupy a spot in independent reading baskets. Once students are taught to re-read to check for meaning and clarity, that practice should be happening throughout the day in every subject. The connections can weave in and out throughout the day. The habits and behaviors of readers are connected to the habits and behaviors of writers—in fact, many are exactly the same!

Writing contributes to both language development and growth in spelling, decoding, and phonemic awareness—all important precursors to learning to read. Writing also provides an incentive for paying thoughtful attention to words. All of this will affect a child's growth in **reading** development.

The connections between reading and writing will remain invisible unless we expose them to our students. This book shows you how to teach those connections. When a young writer makes decisions about how to focus his piece and which details to include, he is practicing determining importance. A writer creates pictures with words, intending his reader to experience the same imagery. These are the connections I am talking about.

We need to notice the obvious link ourselves and to make HUGE the idea that the skills and strategies that students practice to become proficient writers will also nudge them closer to becoming proficient readers. This book will show you how to do that.

Yes, it does sound like common sense: writing and reading are connected. But common sense does not always prevail. One day when my daughter Maddie was three years old, she exited her bedroom ready for ballet class. She had pulled her sparkly pink tights on over her even more sparkly tutu. She looked at me, tights covering her netted tutu and whined in frustration, "I don't look like a real ballerina."

"No, you don't, honey," I replied. "Common sense should tell you that your tights go on underneath your tutu."

She stared at me for a moment, her brow furrowed in thought, and then retorted, "Why should I listen to him? I don't even know who he is."

When it comes to connecting reading and writing, let's listen to common sense. Reading and writing can and should support each other. My hope is that this book will encourage you to begin teaching early writing and reading together and to reflect on some basic questions that can inform your teaching:

- How can I connect the conversations in reading and writing workshop?
- What can I learn about the readers in my classroom through their writing?
- What can my students learn about reading through writing?
- How can I teach young writers to support their readers?
- How can I teach readers how to use a writer's supports intentionally?

How can you use writing to think about and respond to reading in a deep way? Let's begin the exploration.

CHAPTER ONE

The Reciprocal Development of Early Writing and Reading

Writing is the foundation of reading; it may be the most basic way to learn about reading. When writer's read, they use insights they have acquired when they compose. When students write, they learn how reading is put together because they do it. They learn the essence of print.

— *Jane Hansen*

I realized the reciprocal development of early writing and reading when my daughter, Andrea, was two years old. We were waiting in a restaurant for our pepperoni pizza to arrive. Andrea was writing diligently with a crayon, making squiggles and letters on her place mat. I was so excited to see her writing that I couldn't contain the teacher in me. "Ande," I asked. "What does it say?" She looked hard at her writing, held the placemat up to her ear, and then said, with deep concern, "It doesn't say anything!" Ande had no understanding of the connection between writing and reading. I had not built that bridge for her. She had not yet learned the essence of print or the world of a story.

Story, in its broadest sense, is the retelling of a set of events that are related in some way. A story is anything that it is retold or recounted, the telling of a happening that may be true or not true. Sometimes, young children's stories take the form of personal narratives in which they are the main character. Other times, they tell how-to stories that instruct their reader how to make or reenact something. Often, their stories may look like a poem or even a diagram.

Young children have many stories floating around in their heads, and they are usually willing to share the most intimate details with an audience. Their stories might take the form of telling the reader about Mom or a pet. Or the time they lost a tooth, or got lost at the park, or how to make cookies or play soccer.

Talk about what a story is. Discuss how important it is to be able to share stories with other people. Talk with your students about how, when you want to share a story with someone else, you must be able to write, and how, if you want to enjoy a story that someone else has shared, you must be able to read. The reciprocity starts there: the reader and writer can be the same person.

So how does the development of early writing and reading support each other in other ways that are obvious and maybe not so obvious? Let's begin with a child's story.

One day mi bike fil dwn. I hrt my nee.

What does this piece tell us about this child's ability to write and read? Plenty! The evidence of the skills that this child knows is abundant, and it points to definite instructional paths in both writing and reading.

The Student Knows	We know this because the student...	Future writing instruction	Future reading instruction
Concept of word	Uses spaces between words.	Using sounds words.	Reading with expression.
Sight words	Uses *one, day, my, down*.	Writing words that contain an *r*-controlled vowel.	Reading words that contain an *r*-controlled vowel.
Simple sentence structure	Wrote two complete thoughts.	Varied sentence structures.	Fluency.
Story language	Began story with 'One day...'	Telling the inside story-feelings.	Making text to self connections.

For this child, we should compliment the positive behaviors that we see evidenced. She has the concept of how letters go together to make a word because she leaves spaces in between groups of letters. She knows several sight words and can write two complete sentences. From looking at this piece of writing, I can pinpoint some areas of writing instruction for her. For example, she could be taught to use sound words. That would elevate the story in a way that would entertain the reader. She didn't spell *hurt* correctly, so I could teach her about writing *r*-controlled vowels. Finally, I could teach her how to write a compound sentence by putting her two sentences together.

But how would all of this inform my reading instruction? When planning reading instruction, I think about the skill I taught in writing and how the student would apply that skill as a reader. If I had taught her how to write a sound word, during reading I could teach her how to read sound words with expression. If I taught her how to write *r*-controlled vowels I could make the connection for reading *r*-controlled words. Everything you teach in writing will have a connection to reading in some form.

So let's start where it all begins: the alphabetic principle.

The alphabetic principle is defined as the ability to associate sounds with letters and to use these sounds to form words.

The alphabetic principle—necessary for both encoding meaning into written symbols and decoding the information from written symbols—is the basis for both reading and writing. It is the common avenue by which both processes arrive at meaning. As Andrea Butler writes, "Reading and writing are both acts of composing. Readers using their background knowledge and experience to compose meaning from text; writers using their background knowledge and experience compose meaning into text. Children who are better writers tend to be better decoders."

Students need the alphabetic principle in order to encode and decode text. Linnea Ehri's work supports the belief that being able to read words by sight automatically is the key to skilled reading of text. She identified four progressive phases that students move through to attain the ability to decipher words and make meaning of print, and to do both automatically.

Her research showed that emergent readers begin to read by remembering specific letters by their look in the *pre-alphabetic stage*. They move on to the *partial-alphabetic phase,* recognizing some letters because they are familiar, then onto the *full-alphabetic phase,* recognizing letters by sight and by the sound they make, to fluently and automatically putting letters and sounds together in the *consolidated-alphabetic phase.* Understanding this four-phase journey within the context of writing will help you do a better job of integrating writing and reading instruction. As children progress through these stages, their fluency for writing stories will improve. We can encourage practice in the alphabetic principle by prompting students to encode by stretching out words they don't know how to spell slowly and then recording the sounds they hear. We can also encourage practice by prompting students to decode by looking closely at the letters in the words and then matching the sound that the letter stands for.

As students begin to show proficiency in the alphabetic principle, practice will be the key to moving them towards automaticity. As students move through the phases of understanding the relationship between letters and sounds they will also be moving up the phonics continuum. As students master basic consonant sounds they move into learning the vowel sounds. As the teacher, it would help me plan instruction in reading and writing if I knew that my student were able to read some letters by sight and was on at the initial consonant stage on the phonics continuum.

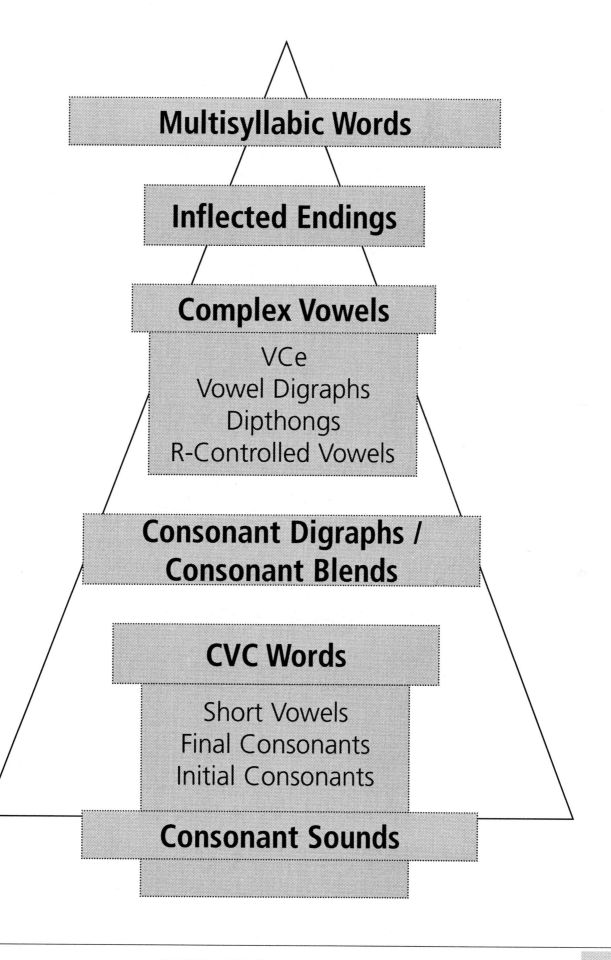

Multisyllabic Words

Inflected Endings

Complex Vowels

VCe
Vowel Digraphs
Dipthongs
R-Controlled Vowels

**Consonant Digraphs /
Consonant Blends**

CVC Words

Short Vowels
Final Consonants
Initial Consonants

Consonant Sounds

Activities to Support the Acquisition of the Alphabetic Principle through Reading and Writing

Pre-Alphabetic Stage:
Students are at the bottom of the phonics continuum.

Student Knows	Needs to Learn	Instructional Stategies
Own name, I, a	20-30 words by sight	Identifying words within a text Writing the same words in own writing
The visual features of some letters	Letters of the alphabet	Use of same alphabet chart for reading and writing. Playing with sounds in words by reading and writing. Sorting letters by various attributes. Place letters on student desk during independent writing. Labeling own sketch with highlighted letters. Use highlighter tape to identify letters in independent reading. Use highlighter tape to identify letters after independent writing.
Some directionality	Top to bottom, left to right	Shared reading Shared writing

Partial-Alphabetic Phase:
Students are at the bottom of the phonics continuum.

Student Knows	Needs to Learn	Instructional Stategies
20-30 sight words	50-100 sight words	Word wall activities during reading and writing. 1.Spell and Chant 2. Sort the words 3. Guess the word 4. Rainbow writing 5. Word Wall Bingo
Some beginning sounds	All letter/sound correspondence	Stretching words to blend the sounds. Stretching words to record sounds. Re-read to check words.
How to write most letters slowly	How to write all letters fluently	Write on white boards. Write in the air. Label sketches. Trace words in shared reading books.
Can guess words using context and partial letter cues	To read words by analogy	Practice reading words using analogy during shared and independent reading. Practice writing words using analogy during shared and independent writing.

Full-Alphabetic Phase:
Students are in the middle of the phonics continuum.

Student Knows	Needs to Learn	Instructional Activities
Short vowel patterns, silent *e*, diagraphs, blends	Vowel teams, dipthongs, *r*-controlled vowels, syllable patterns	Word sorts. Stretching and writing big words. Using what they know in reading about a word to write the word.
Reads word by word	Fluency of 60-70 words per minute	Partner reading. Re-reading authored and self-authored text.
100 sight words	200 sight words	Center activities involving word study. Independent reading and writing.
How to sound out a word	How to look through an entire word	Cross checking to make sure the word looks right, sounds right, and makes sense.

Consolidated-Alphabetic Phase:
Students are at the top of the phonics continuum.

Student Knows	Needs to Learn	Activities to Teach
100 sight words	150-200 sight words	Word sorts. Editing checklists Making big words.
Recognizes one syllable word patterns-top of phonics continuum	Syllable combining	Using known syllables from multiple words to decode bigger words. (Ex. *pen* in *penny* could help decode *pencil*.)
Basic vocabulary words	More variety in word choice	Using antonyms, synonyms, compound words.
Reading/writing in phrases	Compound sentences, phrases	Reader's Theatre. Exposure to different media.

Richard Gentry (1981) and many others have identified four stages of beginning spelling. Gentry's stages include *pre-communitive, semiphonetic, phonetic, transitional,* and *conventional*. Pre-communitive spellers use pictures and letters to spell words. Semiphonetic spellers use temporary spelling where some sounds are represented but not all. The phonetic speller represents all sounds, and the transitional speller uses knowledge of vowels and consonants but does not always spell with correct vowel rules. Finally, the conventional speller uses mostly correct spelling.

These stages are all interrelated and can be used with the stages of acquisition of the alphabetic principle and the phonics continuum to guide instruction. We can get triple use of our instructional time when we analyze the reading and writing of our student while keeping all of these stages in mind.

The chart on page 11 places these stages alongside the stages for reading and writing development. Knowing where students display strengths will help you know where to build. For example, if I have a student who is in the early writing stage but still has many confusions about how to retell a familiar storybook, I could use his own writing as a springboard for helping him understand how a story might go even if he isn't the author. Perhaps I have another student who is in the phonetic stage of spelling but follows me around during writing workshop exclaiming, "How do you spell?" I would know that this child certainly has the capability to be an early writer, she just needs some explicit instruction on how all she knows about letter-sound correspondence will help her write her own story.

These stages are not always clear-cut. Students will move in and out of stages as they approximate learning. The important thing to remember is to make the connection for young readers and writers: what you are learning in one area of literacy will always serve you well in another area.

The Related Development of the Alphabetic Principle, Spelling, Reading, and Writing

Alphabetic Principle	Spelling	Reading	Writing
Pre-alphabetic Totally unaware of how print works in reading and writing.	**Precommunitive** Uses random pictures and letters.	**Emergent** Enjoys listening to books and retelling familiar storybooks.	**Emergent** Tells stories orally, sketches to remember how story goes.
Partial-alphabetic Reads words by forming connections between some of the letters. Knows most letters and sounds.	**Semiphonetic** Some letter sound correspondence, often leaves out vowels.	**Early** Building a sight word base, less reliance on rhyme and repetition, beginning to read in phrases.	**Early** Writes at least two complete thoughts with beginning and some ending sounds.
Full-alphabetic Knows all letters and sounds plus some irregularities, can use word chunks to cross check, reading still not fluent.	**Phonetic** Represents all sounds. Some blends and diagraphs appear.	**Transitional** Reads longer text, beginning to use cueing systems independently to self-monitor.	**Transitional** Writes three complete thoughts with elaboration and a beginning and ending. Uses temporary spelling and sight words.
Consolidated alphabetic Has a large sight word vocabulary, uses analogies, suffixes, prefixes.	**Transitional** Uses structural elements, (syllables, inflectional endings, affixes, uses vowel in every syllable.	**Fluent** Less reliance on illustrations, appropriate pacing and prosody, cross-checks using all strategies.	**Beginning** Writes a story with a beginning, middle, and end. Mostly correct spelling and simple punctuation.
	Conventional Uses correct spelling, Use spelling rules and historical roots.	**Advanced** Reads to learn using a large variety of genre.	**Intermediate** Writes multiple paragraphs with a organizational pattern, sentence variety, spelling, punctuation.

I once heard Lucy Calkins, who has published extensively about the connection between reading and writing, share her confusion about the decisions school districts were making about classroom schedules: with additional time needed to prepare students for high stakes reading tests, writing time was being decreased. What a mistake!

Teaching reading and writing simultaneously results in increased reading achievement. Writing lets you explore what you know, recognize what you don't know and highlight what you would like to know more about. It is through writing that we become conscious of our thinking. Reading builds up knowledge and writing extends it.

In *One on One*, Calkins, Hartman, and White write, "The writing workshop provides beginning readers with a powerful context for developing their reading as well as their writing skills. Actually, approximately half of the time that beginning readers invest in a piece of writing is spent on reading rather than writing."

As students become more proficient encoders of their own stories, they can begin to turn their attention towards comprehension. When students learn why they must include a letter for every sound heard in a word, leave spaces between words, punctuate appropriately, and write neatly, they are on their way to understanding that the purpose of writing and reading is the same—to share information in a way that makes sense!

We should use what we see students doing during both literacy processes. Observing writing and reading behaviors will help you provide an instructional plan that uses reading and writing lessons to support and inform each other.

Noticing what students attempt as they try to write words should guide our reading instruction. We need to use what we see our students using or misusing as they attempt to decode unknown words to guide our instruction in writing. There are so many ways to build the connection throughout the day.

Depending on their phase of development, you can share a pen to strengthen the connection between letters and sounds, or write in tandem. Point out words on the word wall that students can write lickity-split. Remind them often that these words do not need to be stretched out. Practice on white boards during small group. Remind students of familiar structures enjoyed during shared reading and encourage students to try these with group support first before giving it a go on their own. A repeating line or a list-with-a-twist will serve as a strong scaffold for budding writers. Publish small-group stories on chart paper and allow students to revisit these pieces for inspiration. Keeping a record of phonics development with writing samples will support your work during reading as well as writing instruction. Design a grid or checklist to identify where your students are on the phonics continuum. Begin with recording initial consonants, final consonants, initial consonant blends, digraphs, vowels, short and long, word families, inflected endings and finally ending blends and digraphs. Try conferring with the same student in reading and writing. This will help you target your instruction and get double mileage in addressing specific trouble areas in phonics. These are the lessons that connect reading and writing.

Observable Behaviors in Reading and Writing

As a behavior emerges in one process, instruct students of how it relates to the reciprocal process. This type of quick assessment will assist you in teaching into areas students are using but confusing. If you witness these behaviors in both reading and writing, chances are the student has reached mastery. For example, if a student writes with letter/sound correspondence, he should also be able to read with letter/sound correspondence. If he can't, knowing which area he's stronger in, reading or writing, will serve as a scaffold for instruction.

Phonemic Awareness

Writing	Reading
Segments words into individual sounds.	Segments words into individual sounds.
Moves letters to represent identified sounds.	Positions mouth to read identified sounds.
Writes with letter/sound correspondence.	Reads with letter/sound correspondence.

Phonics

Writing	Reading
Recognizes and writes all letter names and sounds.	Reads letters according to identified sounds.
Writes with beginning, medial, and final consonant sounds.	Reads through the entire word.
Writes using blends and digraphs.	Reads words containing blends and digraphs.
Writes using vowels.	Reads vowels correctly.

Vocabulary

Writing	Reading
Writes with more challenging words.	Understands words with multiple meanings.
Uses a dictionary and thesaurus appropriately.	Understands the purpose of a dictionary and thesaurus in comprehending text.
Purposely writes with context clues.	Uses context clues to figure out unfamiliar words.
Writes using synonyms.	Comprehends synonyms with intention.

Fluency

Writing	Reading
Writes sight words fluently.	Reads sight words fluently
Re-reads to check fluency.	Re-reads to fix fluency.
Writes in meaningful phrases.	Reads in phrases.
Reads own writing with intonation.	Reads text with intonation.

Comprehension

Writing	Reading
Writes from personal experience.	Uses background knowledge to make sense of text.
Writes to 'show, not tell.'	Visualizes to make meaning.
Writes with a purposeful structure.	Identifies text structure to make predictions about the text.
Determines importance for the reader.	Retells with consideration for importance.

Showing students how these processes support each other will enable them to become flexible problem-solvers of print. The mini-lessons in the second half of this book will assist you in delivering lessons that will be taught during writing workshop but will support reading through the reciprocity.

The Three Shared Cueing Systems of Writing and Reading

As young writers and readers move along the continuum from emergent to accomplished processors of text, several information sources should supply cues that help them elicit meaning from print. These are called cueing systems, sources of information, or working systems. These are the areas that allow every reader to make sense of print. A reader or writer who is working independently automatically attends to one or more of these cues in text. These cueing systems include *meaning* (or *semantic*) cues; *structural* (or *syntactical*) cues; and *graphophonic* (or *visual*) cues.

These cueing systems provide a powerful connection between the processes of writing and reading. When **readers** use these cueing systems they are **decoding** text; when **writers** use them, they are **encoding**. Both reading and writing require the fluent and automatic use of these cueing systems. Practice supports and strengthens facility with the cueing systems whether the student is engaged in reading or writing.

Meaning cues emerge from the student's background knowledge and understanding of the message. In reading, the message comes from the author, an outside source. In writing, this message comes from within, from the writer himself. Meaning cues in both reading and writing require the question, "Does this make sense?"

Structural cues derive from control of oral language and exposure to book language. In reading, the structure involves the proper use of grammar (including tenses, endings, and irregular verbs). Because very young children approximate so much of their language, this sometimes causes confusion when learning to make a story "sound like you talk." In writing, the structure provides support for the reader who must decipher the words. Structural cues in both cases require the question, "Does it sound right?"

Graphophonic cues come from the alphabetic principle. While reading, a student attends to the visual components of a letter and matches it with the sound that letter stands for. When the reader makes a successful match she is decoding, and the graphophonic cue system is working for her. An emergent writer uses graphophonic cues when slowly stretching out an unknown word to register the letters that represent those sounds in a process known as encoding. Whether decoding or encoding, the writer and the reader both ask themselves the same question: "Does this look right?" In fact, acquisition of the features of the written code become much more obvious when a child attempts to puts his ideas in writing for someone else to read, than when he tries to read someone else's ideas. We can actually see the graphophonic system being used when he segments a word and records the sounds.

Successful readers and writers orchestrate all of the cueing systems automatically as they read or write. They are free to focus on the meaning of the words. These high-progress readers operate on print with high accuracy and high self-correction rates. Similarly, high-process writers notice that sounds in speech can be written in consistent ways, thus empowering them to write any word—not just sight words—to put their messages on paper. The true focus of our instruction comes from the words of Frank Smith who reminds us that our students must "write like readers and read like writers."

CHAPTER TWO

Basics for Creating the Writing/ Reading-Connected Classroom

Remember: Storytelling can lead to storywriting and reading.

— *Dale Gordon*

Our days consist of endless events that join together to become the stories of our lives. However, children don't necessarily know that the trip to the park or the beautiful butterflies that decorate a garden will become the basis for their stories. We need to teach them that these small moments can be recalled at any time and then shared through print. They have to be taught how to send these moments out into the world to be enjoyed by others.

In my primary classroom, I often encourage students to share their stories, and am always haunted when they reply, "I don't have anything to write about." During book introductions, I frequently receive blank stares when I ask, "So tell me everything you know about this topic." Far too often, young readers and writers don't believe that they know anything about the world. It is our job to remind them that they do. We must show them where to find their stories. The knowledge that stories are everywhere will support them as they grow as readers and writers.

Often knowing where to begin is the most difficult. Shared class experiences are perfect as models when showing students how to get a story out of their head and into the air. This chapter will walk you through ways to get your own class story going.

The Importance of Oral Storytelling

Effective communication must include both oral and reading vocabulary, and beginning readers will use their own oral vocabulary to make sense of the words they see in print. Class stories will allow students to develop deliberate vocabulary that supports meaning and can be used as a scaffold for their own stories. Oral storytelling is an art form that has been lost in many primary classrooms. If we want students to share the stories in their heads, then we have to provide the forum for teaching them how to speak and how to listen. By taking for granted that our students are masters these skills, we miss our first opportunity to make the connection between reading and writing visible.

For our youngest students, reading and writing first connect in spoken language. We want children to be in touch with their own speaking and listening because negotiating meaning is the way young children learn about the world. If we think about literacy in any form, the making of meaning is always the goal. We know the most fundamental way to make meaning is through speaking and listening and that oral language in the early grades is highly connected with reading comprehension in the upper grades. So it seems the connection between writing and reading begins with oral language.

Because so many children enter kindergarten with poorly developed oral language skills, it seems smart to start at the beginning by developing our students' ability to speak and to listen. Some lucky children have over 1,000 hours of literacy experience prior to kindergarten; others arrive with as few as five (Adams, 1990). It is important that we close the vocabulary gap by providing opportunities for children to develop and practice their language skills. An often-missed opportunity is the shared oral class story.

The class story conveys many foundational skills that apply to later reading and writing: Children learn that their stories matter. They learn how to speak and to listen so they can reenact a story. Once a shared class experience is identified, you can model the narrative structure, composing it in the air, determining out loud what ideas to use and which to discard. Academic language that incorporates talking like a writer is practiced during oral storytelling as students incorporate vocabulary and structure that will serve them well as readers and writers.

Class stories also provide a common ground for English Language Learners and students with suppressed language abilities. As students begin to contribute to a class story, they draw on their pre-existing knowledge of narrative structure and vocabulary. All students will grow their own knowledge from a common ground of a shared class story. As the story grows and changes, students can practice oral revision in a safe, scaffolded environment. They will be more motivated and willing to take a risk with language. Because an oral retelling of their own story is embedded in an authentic literacy experience, their level of language proficiency will grow.

Telling a story out loud is a perfect way to model the connection between writing and reading. When a person tells a story, it's important to include the setting and enough details so that the listener can follow along. These are necessary decisions in writing as well. Storytellers constantly make decisions about what information to include in the text and what information to leave for the reader to infer. Listeners—and readers—envision themselves in the story, integrating personal background knowledge with the details that the storyteller—or author—provides. The writing/reading processes are reciprocal, and are made accessible to the youngest readers and writers by telling the story out loud.

It is natural to revise a story each time it is told. We have all heard someone tell a story in which the fish caught on a vacation grows each time the story is told, until the barely-big-enough-to-keep fish becomes so large it could feed a family of ten. Each time that story was told, it was revised. We definitely don't want to encourage our students to become tellers of tall tales, but it is very natural in oral language to change the story as we speak. We need to take advantage of this natural tendency and use it to develop vocabulary and facility with the structure of English, knowing that those skills will be transferred into print later. The story teller becomes the story writer.

Oral storytelling also provides immediate feedback—reaction from the audience about how well our story is comprehended. The faces of the members of the audience tell us right away if there is confusion in the story, providing an authentic and valuable teaching point for young writers and readers. Oral storytelling provides the scaffold and model for many of the processes applicable to process writing. It is an important step that is often left out.

As students begin to tell the stories of their lives they will begin to view themselves as "people to whom things happen." Their personal oral stories will become background knowledge for comprehending the stories they will read, and the basis for the stories they will later write.

After you're sure that the students feel successful with telling the class story out loud, the story can be transferred to print. Because the meaning is already in working memory, the ability to write and then re-read the class story is enhanced.

It's a good idea to repeat the oral to print storytelling process throughout the year. The repeated practice of telling a story out loud will lift students' language skills, develop their sense of personal narrative, and build a classroom literacy community. To that end, it's helpful to keep a class list of topics that could become a class story. The list reminds students they can help choose a new story, and that you expect them to keep searching for new story ideas.

Oral Storytelling and the Writing/Reading Connection

Many opportunities for literacy learning are tucked into all this storytelling! For example, you can remind your class of how much their story sounds like a story you would read in a book. You can discuss the sequence of the story, the characters, the events, or the meaning and mood of the story. You can begin to point out writing-craft elements such as a hook, ending, or transition.

Jerome Brunner (1993) writes that "proficiency in oral language provides children with a vital tool for thought. Without fluent and structured oral language, children will find it very difficult to think." Oral storytelling precedes the written story and provides explicit practice in all seven components of our language system that Louisa Moats identified in 2000:

- *phonology* or the basic sound units
- *morphology* or units of meaning within word
- *syntax* or sentence structure
- *semantics* or the way language conveys meaning
- *pragmatics* or the appropriate word choice and use
- *orthography* or spelling patterns
- *vocabulary* or the knowledge of the meaning and pronunciation of words

Oral language is the place where the writing/reading connection begins. If we miss the opportunity for students to share their story orally before taking it to print, we are doing them a terrible disservice. Speaking, listening, reading, and writing are mutually enhancing, interdependent activities that should be advanced without a hierarchy of value. They are all essential and should be taught simultaneously. Sharing and exploring stories with each other will build community and reinforce that conveying meaning begins with the storyteller.

How to Incorporate Storytelling into Your Teaching Day

Find the Time

Oral storytelling should be an integral part of the school day. I realize that finding the time to "tell stories" is not always easy. I suggest using writing workshop time during the early part of the school year for sharing a class story. Storytelling can begin on the first day of school. Gather your students at the end of the day and tell the story of one event. For example, the story of how everyone came cautiously in the door looking carefully for their nametags or how they walked quietly to lunch make great first day stories. I began writer's workshop with storytelling for the first month of school. During the first ten minutes of workshop, I told stories of my youth and invited my students to share their stories as well. Although these stories were often fragmented or went on and on, we took turns and got to know each other. I learned that Kristin had twin brothers who teased her and that Bobby broke his arm rollerblading. We began to build a community through story. I tried to sneak time for storytelling before or after lunch, at the end of the day, or quickly while lining up for specials. Even though the events and experiences my students were sharing during this time weren't always stories, I was setting the stage for what was to come: our shared class story.

By providing this time, students will learn how to plan and sequence a story, try out words, and practice clarity. And they will gain the confidence that their stories are important to tell and that every moment in their life is important.

Choose a Class Topic

Finding a story that belongs to the class presents your students with a challenge. This will be **the** story that will sustain them for a month. The story they choose could be about the time you all found the caterpillar on the sidewalk on the way to lunch, or the new window just installed in the lunchroom, or the bus ride to see the farm. The topic isn't as important as the fact that the event is shared by everyone in the class. Whether you chose the time you lost your keys or the first fire drill, find the topic that will be "your story." This story will provide an important framework and should be one that everyone can contribute and enjoy together.

Tell the Story

Call the class to the gathering area. It should be a large-enough space so students can sit in a circle and see each other. Begin the story by saying, "Readers and writers, our words become stories when we put them together to share a special memory. We have looked around carefully and have found our first class story. It is very important to share our story clearly so that our audience will feel like they are in the moment with us. So today we are going to practice telling our story. We are going to tell our story many times and when we are ready to put it out into the world we can invite others in to hear our story. Okay, I will tell the story today and you listen to make sure I am telling it clearly."

Tell the story bit by bit, slowly, and with expression. Natalie Louis, a staff developer with the Reading and Writing Project at Columbia University has her students hold their hands like books and they pretend to turn the page at the appropriate times.

A class story might begin like this:

"One day on our way to lunch we saw butterflies in the garden. (Turn the page.) They were everywhere, blue ones, yellow ones, and orange ones. (Turn the page.) Kiera said, 'Look at all the butterflies.' (Turn the page.) We all stopped quietly on the sidewalk to watch them. (Turn the page.) They were fluttering from flower to flower. (Turn the page.) They looked like they were playing tag. (Turn the page.) We wish we could have joined them. (Close the book.)"

This class story will become the foundation for playing with words, sentences, and phrases. Having a class conversation will extend your students' thinking by giving them the time to practice vocabulary skills, sequencing, and retelling.

Tell the Story Again

After you've told the story exactly the same way several times over a few days, begin to involve the class. I always found it helpful to write the story down verbatim the first time I told it so I would remember. From the very beginning, enlist every child in pretending to have a book in front of them, turning imaginary pages on your cue. Then, begin the story, but ask a volunteer to share the next page. Remember to continue having students pretend to turn the page after each event. Encourage the students to check for narrative order. If a student shares his page out of correct sequence, point it out and ask the student to think back carefully and decide what really happened next. Tell the story at least once a day.

Mix the Story Up

After students become very familiar with the story, you can help them begin to play with it. Retell the story, but change at least one of the elements described below. As you do, you will be introducing your young writers and readers to revision and the specific writing-craft Target Skills® they should have at their command to make their later written pieces stronger.

"Today, readers and writers, we are going to...

- begin with a sound word
- end with a quote
- use dialogue
- slow this one part way down
- start in the middle and tell the story from there
- use a different word for *said*
- try a repeating line
- show, not tell our favorite page
- use proper names
- add internal thinking
- change our story into a 'how-to' piece
- change our story into a poem
- write a circular ending
- use a sketch to tell our story

Tell the Story to a Partner

Now it's time to ask students to work together with a partner. It's good to match a very verbal child with one who is only moderately so. Timid children should be matched with a moderately verbal child as well. Avoid partnerships in which one child will totally dominate the storytelling time. Telling the class story to a partner can last anywhere from two days to a month. When students are ready to move to a new class story, move on. However, it is always fun to return to an old favorite to retell to a partner.

Invite students first to tell the story together, reminding them to turn the page as appropriate. Then work towards one child telling the story to the other.

Share the Story with an Audience

When students are very familiar with the class story in whole group and in partnerships, return to the whole group with the purpose of sharing the story with the world. Invite someone in to hear it. This could be the principal, the media specialist, the cafeteria supervisor, a parent—anyone! You could also take the show on the road and tell the story to another classroom or on the school news channel.

Take the Story to Print

Once the class story has become an old favorite, it can be taken to print. The teacher should write the story on chart paper and then present it to the class. Choral read the class story and check for focus and clarity. Revise if necessary and then leave the story posted for all to enjoy. It is always fun to return to an old class story to enjoy during shared reading or literacy centers. From time to time, the class story could be published in book form, with members of the class acting as illustrators.

Don't expect that students will write this story themselves. The purpose of this type of oral storytelling is to develop a sense of how a story goes, and how it sounds in the air. As students hear and tell more stories, they will be more successful with writing stories. Right now, telling the story coherently with expression and prosody is the goal.

Tell Your Own Story

Later in the year, after much practice with a class story, students can begin to tell their own stories much like they did during the first weeks of school. Now, however, their stories should be focused in a narrative style that engages the listener. These will become the stories that students can take to print.

An Oral Storytelling Timeline

Day One

Choose your class story. The teacher tells the story while the class listens in and pretends to turn the page.

Days Two through Four

Teacher tells the story with students sharing some of the pages.

Day Five through Seven

Teacher begins the story and students tell the rest.

Days Eight through Twelve

Teachers make suggestion for how the students can revise the story. Students retell the story with that focus with a partner.

Days Twelve through Thirteen

Return to whole group to practice the story. Invite others in to hear the story or take the story to another class to share.

Day Fourteen

Take the story to print. Choral read or publish in book form.

Day Fifiteen

Choose a new story and begin the process again.

Note: As students become proficient at whole-class storytelling, begin to allow time for individual storytelling.

Developing Vocabulary Deliberately

Children experiment with words orally before they can write. Most families tell special stories about those early tries with vocabulary. My own daughter, for example, was convinced she was going to have her ears *peered* instead of *pierced* and would only eat her hamburger *weldon* instead of *well-done*. It seems logical to expect that children will experiment with written vocabulary in the same way.

Writing provides an ideal opportunity for primary children to practice and play with words. In fact, mucking about with words is the essence of writing. A child has fun being the boss of his own words. Teaching students how to express themselves with their words is a worthy goal. Writers don't have the luxury of gestures, facial expressions, vocal cues, or the interactions that speakers use to gauge and convey meaning. Therefore writing provides the incentive for paying close attention to language in order to find the words to get meaning across (Sheffenbine, 2007). Recognizing that trait in other authors should be a daily mission.

As teachers, we should remember that children must be exposed to thousands and thousands of words in order to build a vocabulary from which they can find just the "right" word when speaking and writing. By reading aloud and creating time in our day to discuss words and what they mean, we grow a knowledge base of words for our students. Encouraging students to use words that bring a sentence alive will serve them well not only in reading but in every aspect of their lives.

Studying the meanings of words and developing vocabulary is important for both writing and reading. I have already noted that knowledge of word meanings is a powerful predictor of reading comprehension. We know that children's vocabularies develop by engagement in oral language, listening to adults talk with them, being read to and reading on their own. We also know that explicit vocabulary instruction is often slighted in the primary grades in order to provide more time for other literacy areas, such as phonics and word identification skills.

Recent research has shown that vocabulary and language skills are to a considerable degree quite separate from skills leading to word identification skills (Biemiller and Boote, 2006). Because the reading instruction targeted at emergent readers usually involves text with little challenging vocabulary, it is necessary to supplement vocabulary instruction in order for students to gain the 1,000 word-meanings a year needed for successful comprehension after grade two (Biemiller and Boote, 2006). Encouraging students to tell and then write their own stories provides an effective supplement to vocabulary instruction. We know teaching vocabulary in context is more effective than no-context instruction. Context of your own design—for example, the story of something that actually happened to you—is very effective.

Writing workshop provides a ripe opportunity for establishing new words. Students must think of words as a painter does paint. Crafting sentences with specifically chosen words enlarges vocabulary that assists with comprehension. Carey (1978) suggests that new words can be mapped to verbal narrative context and then extended as the word is encountered in other contexts. Children learn words by engaging in life experiences and talking about these experiences using familiar vocabulary. In turn, a direct explanation of a synonym or a multiple word meaning to map onto the familiar vocabulary will have an impact on his vocabulary. For example, if a child encounters the word *happy* either in his own writing or in other connected text and is given the word *ecstatic* as a word that means a higher degree of happy, the child will have a greater chance of using and understanding *ecstatic* in his writing and reading. Mini-lessons that specifically teach word choice with reoccurring emphasis on word meaning along with the opportunity to use words in a meaningful way will support vocabulary acquisition. Students can take much more responsibility for building their own vocabulary in a supportive classroom that links reading and writing. We must not accept mediocrity in word choice, even in our youngest writers.

Paper as a Writing/Reading Scaffold

We've all experimented with different types of writing paper for our young writers to use—journals, newsprint, handwriting paper, blank paper—you name it. Some classes respond well to writing a page a day in spiral-bound notebooks. Many teachers, including me, primarily used monthly journals made up of blank pieces of paper stapled together.

However, I noticed that every time I gave students some special type of paper I would get back a different type of writing. I began experimenting by preparing different pieces of paper: I would include a picture box, or a template for a list or a personal letter. I soon realized that paper could work like 'just-right books' and support students as they move along the phases of literacy development. A 'just-right book' is one that is not too hard—but not too easy—for students to read independently. Just-right books are right on students' cusp of learning.

Just-right paper works the same way. Paper that supports a writer appropriately will allow them to put more effort into making meaning. I discovered that my students were more successful with paper that did not have too many lines, or too few lines, but just the right number of lines.

Because of my experiments, I realized that paper is, indeed, a very important but often overlooked scaffold for the young writer/reader at every phase of literacy development. Pre-bound journals have a place, but you should provide other supports as well—paper scaffolds that recognize, and match with, the literacy phase of the child. The five templates on pages 29-33 provide those scaffolds.

Paper Template One (see page 29) provides a natural bridge between the spoken and the written word for the early-phase writers/readers who struggle to remember how a story goes. When we teach them to think about their story and then sketch the whole story first, the visual representation serves as a place holder for the meaning. Sketching is an important step in writing. Just as we encourage students to derive clues from the illustrations in the books they are reading, the sketch in their own writing can provide clues as well. The sketch represents the ideas, events, and feelings of the author and can be used as the meaning-holder. As young writers use their sketch to retell their story orally, it provides the scaffold for remembering how the story goes. A sketch is a quick representational drawing that serves as the place-holder for the writing. It is not an illustration with full color. Students will have to be taught through a mini-lesson the difference.

As students become more proficient at sketching their stories on one sheet of paper, they could move to stretching the story out across several pages. Just as we teach students in reading to take a picture walk, we should also teach them to picture-walk through writing their own stories. The simply formatted piece of paper in **Paper Template Two** (see page 30) helps them do that as well as add a line of print.

As students become more comfortable with sketching and recording beginning sounds, they can begin to practice stretching out entire words and recording all sounds by labeling the important parts of their sketch. **Paper Template Three** (see page 31) has room for an adequate picture box that will encourage young writers at this phase to include a sketch, a label, and a sentence. By only including one or two lines, the idea of writing the story is not so overwhelming.

Paper Template Four (see page 32) supports the development of young writers who are moving from words to writing several sentences. The picture box and several lines invite the writer to use their labels to create sentences about their sketch.

As they develop the ability to write more, the number of lines should increase. **Paper Template Five** (see page 33) encourages growing writers to tell one story with elaboration across several pages. The small sketch box remains as a meaning holder while the large spaces between the lines make it easier for the young writers to revise for craft elements as they add or substitute words, add pages, or even add a cover.

Encourage each child to keep the loose pieces of paper in a two-pocket folder. One side holds ongoing work that needs revision or editing; the other finished work. Every month, students can review and admire their work, choose one to edit, and then publish in some way.

Don't be afraid to develop paper to support the genre you are teaching. If you are teaching your students to write poetry, provide paper that supports line breaks. If you are encouraging students to use a repeating line, design paper that includes special lines just for the repeating phrase. Paper is one way to support meaning for our young readers and writers. Lessons 9 and 10 in the Foundational Mini-lesson section use paper specifically designed to support the focus skill.

Using a variety of paper choices will allow students to re-read their own writing with ease, using the support of the sketch as practiced with illustrations during independent reading.

★ _____

(blank box)

_____

_____

_____

* _____

[blank box]

_____

_____

_____

_____

_____

_____

★ _____

[blank box]

_____

_____

_____

_____

_____

_____

_____

_____

_____

CHAPTER THREE

Teaching a Writing/ Reading Workshop

Because children learn best from explicit, systematic instruction within a predictable structure, a successful workshop should include three distinct parts: the mini-lesson, independent practice, and conferring and a teaching share. The writer's workshop structure recommended here supports Brian Cambourne's widely accepted conditions of learning. The following chart shows how his conditions relate to a classroom that focuses on literacy engagement and the writing/reading connection.

Cambourne's Conditions in the Literacy-Focused Classroom

Immersion: Students are saturated with literacy experiences.

- Classroom provides a print-rich environment with charts, labels, words.
- Read alouds with accountable talk are held.
- Instruction includes author studies, field trips, and living a literate life.

Demonstration: Teacher models literate behaviors, formally and informally.

- Instruction includes a connection, teaching point with demonstration, active engagement, and link.
- Processes are modeled as well as outcomes.
- Students see teacher engaged in reading and writing.

Expectation: Students believe that they can and will be readers and writers.

- Students held accountable for what has been taught.
- Students identify and practice the behaviors of good readers and writers.
- Everyone participates.

Responsibility: Students choose what they will 'try out' as readers and writers as they are continuing immersed in literacy that is 'just-right' for individual gain.

- Students are taught to make appropriate choices.
- There can be no opting out of workshop.
- Students must show responsibility to their partners.

Approximations: Students approximate literacy behaviors at their own level of development. They don't use all aspects of literacy appropriately before attempting to use what they do know.

- Instruction includes the celebration of all steps taken towards the goals of reading and writing.
- Students build on the known.
- Value is placed on the process, not just the finished product.
- Partnerships.
- Mastery learning not expected.

Employment: Students have the opportunity to use and practice what they are learning alone and with others.

- Instruction includes the explicit connection of reading and writing.
- Teacher provides many, many opportunities to practice and apply literacy skills and strategies.
- New learnings linked to previous learnings.

Response: Feedback.

- Sharing.
- Conferring.
- Celebration of all work.

Engagement: Students actively participate in literacy activities.

- Students work with individual book baskets or baggies.
- Students use individual writing folders.
- Teacher provides a risk free environment and time to practice lessons.
- Students choose their topics.
- Students choose just-right books and just-right paper.
- Students work in partnerships.

Workshops provide the foundation for Cambourne's conditions to occur. A workshop by definition is a place where raw materials are used to build something. Within a writing/reading workshop, materials—paper, pencils, and books—are made available along with explicit instruction, demonstration, time to practice, and guiding feedback. A workshop can be framed toward reading or writing but no matter the stated focus of the workshop, both literary processes will in fact be practiced: As students engage in the independent *reading* portion of the workshop, they will be using their knowledge of letter/sound correspondence, visualizing, re-reading for meaning, and bringing background knowledge into the text. As students engage in independent *writing* portion of the workshop, they will be relying on these same strategies.

The beauty of workshops is that they provide a designated time for differentiated practice. Workshops provide time for students to build on all daily components of instruction. During workshops, you should watch for—and encourage—flexibility in how your students use what they know as readers to support their writing, and vice versa. If labeling a sketch with important words was taught during writing workshop, students should be expected to use that same Target Skill during reading workshop to determine anchor words in a text. Workshop provides the venue for teaching reciprocity and then reinforcing the Target Skills during both reading and writing.

The simplicity of workshop teaching is that it looks the same for either reading or writing. A workshop generally consists of a 45 minute chunk of time designated to instruct and practice Target Skills. Workshops should always begin with students in a designated gathering area where the teacher is up front and very close.

The Three Parts of a Workshop

A successful workshop should include three main parts: *the mini-lesson, independent practice with conferring*, and *sharing*. The lessons provided in this book are written to be taught as mini-lessons during writing workshop. However, many of these lessons would be applicable to reading workshop as well. Each lesson has a direct link to reading and could be reinforced using connected text. The independent practice during reading workshop would include listening for students applying the target skill in their reading. Conferring during a reading workshop would include reminders of the similar work done during writing workshop. For example, if my target skill during that day's writing workshop was talking with a partner about my writing, I could use the same mini-lesson during reading workshop and change my target skill to talking to my partner about my reading. The behaviors of a successful partnership—as well as appropriate conversational stems—would be the same. Because the format of the workshop remains the same during both processes, the connections between independent reading and writing are more authentic and are easier to make.

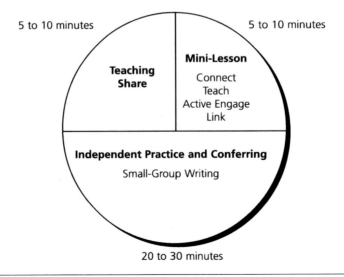

5 to 10 minutes · 5 to 10 minutes

Teaching Share

Mini-Lesson
Connect
Teach
Active Engage
Link

Independent Practice and Conferring
Small-Group Writing

20 to 30 minutes

A reading or writing workshop generally lasts forty-five minutes. Each should contain a *mini-lesson* which should include a *connection, teaching point, active engagement*, and *link to future work*. The mini-lesson should be followed by *independent practice with conferring*, and a short and focused *teacher share*.

Remember that the mini-lesson is your lesson plan for one day's writing instruction. The explicit instruction in the first four steps should not last more than fifteen minutes and should function to focus your teaching and allow you to clearly express the point of the lesson and how to apply it in their own writing and reading. The mini-lesson should be determined by your state and district standards and the needs of your class. These lessons should provide the skills and strategies needed to assist students in becoming literate. The intent of this explicit instruction is for students to internalize this skill and be able to use it flexibly. While the mini-lesson should be directed towards the majority of your class, we know there will be students who will need more scaffolding.

The Mini-Lesson

The *connection* provides students with a reminder of how their previous work in reading or writing will fit with the new learning introduced that day. You should tell students what you will be teaching them, and talk about how this lesson will fit into the work they have been doing, and how it will all fit into their lives as readers and writers. You might say, for example, "Writers, yesterday we were practicing listening and recording sounds in words by stretching them out slowly. But I have noticed there are some words you all can write faster because you already know how to spell them." Or "Readers, yesterday we were practicing retelling our books to our partners. Today we are going to use our fingers as an organizer to help us remember the important parts of our books so that we can share them with our partner."

During the *teaching point* portion, the teacher states explicitly, "Today I am going to teach you _____ because _____." This is the teaching point. We teach students something we hope they'll use often. We do this by demonstrating a strategy or retelling or reenacting something we have done or seen others do in their reading or writing. Demonstrate by showing students how to do it right then and there while they are sitting in front of you. Then remind them of what they saw. You might say, "Today I want to teach you how you can switch back and forth from writing words slowly by stretching them out and writing some words faster because you already know how to write them." Or you might say, "Today I want to teach you how to look through each word carefully to make sure that you have said the sound for each letter."

You should include a modeling of the Target Skill and (usually) a teacher think-aloud as another type of student support. Other techniques you can incorporate into the teaching point section include the use of a shared experience (like in the oral storytelling), a shared read-aloud or class-written story, a piece of children's literature, or a student- or teacher-written model.

You might model with your own story how you write some words quickly because they are words you already know by sight and then how you have to stretch some words out. Think aloud as you write the beginning sentence of your story, switching back and forth between known and unknown words. Or you might read a big book and make note of the structure. You might say, "I noticed that the author asked a question on the first page and then spent the rest of the book answering that one question. That question would be a good thing to keep in my head as I read this book because I know that each page is going to be a part of the answer." Whatever your teaching point, model how to use it authentically in reading and writing.

The teaching point section is the most appropriate place to bridge the reading/writing connection. Remind students of the work they have been doing across their day and how it can help them with this new skill or strategy. For example, if you identified a question/answer text structure during that day's reading workshop, then remind students during writing workshop how that structure might work as a choice for their own organization.

The *active engagement* portion of the mini-lesson gives students an opportunity to try out what you've just taught them in a scaffolded, group setting. Because workshop teaching encourages teachers to gather their students on the floor in front of them, students are sitting close, poised to practice with a shared piece of children's literature, a student model, or with a partner.

Keep this in mind: First, you do. Then, students do with your support. Finally, each student does independently. The active engagement comes when students do with your support. This gradual release will help you differientiate instruction during the *conferring* stage. As you watch students try the new skill on the rug with you and in front of you, confusion will become apparent. Keep students who need more support with you. Quickly and efficiently re-teach the mini-lesson before sending those students off to write independently.

If the workshop is reading, you might want to reference work done in writing that would explicitly connect the skill to reading. Or if it is writing workshop, use familiar text to assist the student. For example, if the target skill for writing workshop was how to write with labels and students are experiencing difficulty reading simple label books, show them their own writing and how they authored labels. Assist them as they re-read their own labels before returning to their independent reading to apply the same skill.

Active engagement often calls for student partnerships. Partnerships should be established by the teacher. These will provide students with a venue for talking about the work required of readers and writers. They will also provide you, as teacher, the opportunity to use your own partner to role play your thinking as you make decisions about how you choose the best word or how you use your finger to read through an entire word. Try having student partners conference together to give you advice on changes to make to your sample writing or reading behaviors. Of course, all students love giving their teacher constructive feedback!

Students can turn to their partners and practice Target Skills out loud. Sometimes the partners can share a piece of text or use a shared experience to practice the new work. In reading, it might sound like, "Turn to your partner and share what you're thinking about the main character so far." In writing, it might sound like, "Turn to your partner and tell them what part you think is the most important part of our class story and why." Time for active engagement allows the teacher to listen to see who has understood the teaching point.

Because of the importance partnerships will play—and to make the most out of their partnership time—students should be taught specific conversational stems. (A *conversational stem* is a simple phrase to get students started talking. For example, "Turn and tell your partner the most important part of the story." Or "Have your partner listen to your story and tell you what she thinks is the most important part." Model with a partner how a stem would be used and then have students practice. As stems become internalized students will be able to choose the one that is most appropriate for the information they hope to glean from their partners. Some stems are more sophisticated than others. I would not teach them all at the same time. Choose the stem that supports strategy teaching. Remember these conversations will have to be grown—go slowly but maintain the expectation that children can have deep meaningful conversations that will assist their literacy learning. The value of this partnership talk is that it makes student thinking visible so we can assist when breakdowns occur.)

Explicit mini-lessons (see pages 62 and 63) in how students should behave during their partnerships will assist them in using active engagement wisely. This is important since we want students to be able to talk deeply and with intent about their reading and writing.

I discussed earlier the importance of oral language. Whatever skill we are teaching should be practiced orally as well as in print. If we are teaching students to make connections in order to write the stories of their lives or to make meaning of the text they are reading, it is important to give students time to talk about these connections first. We want students to stop, think, and react in order to monitor comprehension. We can encourage the use of print and comprehension strategies by allowing students to wade through them first using explicit conversational stems. (Specific conversational stems that link writing and reading are explored more clearly on page 48.)

Linking your current instruction to the ongoing independent work for the day's workshop is the final piece of the explicit portion of your workshop time. Ask for a signal from children who are going to try this work today. You want them to commit to giving this new learning an approximated try. Keep students who may need help for a few minutes to make sure they have a plan for independent practice.

As you send your students off to practice independently, you leave them with the clear expectation that what they have learned today should be applied from now on. The new skill will help them every day and they should remember to use it.

The four parts of the mini-lesson should go very quickly. The teaching should be precise and should not require a lot of elaboration. Very simply, you'll remind students of a previous skill or strategy, teach a new one, model how to do it, provide a minute or two for students to give it a go, and then hold them to trying this new tool in their reading or writing. As teachers, our explanations tend to go on and on, hoping that if we say one more thing, our students will suddenly get it. Unfortunately, this doesn't usually work. Being explicit with one simple demonstration tends to produce better results.

Tips on Mini-Lessons (Adapted from the work of Pinellas Writing Project, 2006)

- The connection is the place to remind students of previous work. They will not realize that their learning is layered unless you point it out to them.

- Keep charts simple and student-friendly. Use picture clues and keep charts to no more than four lines.

- Don't use too many examples. Our students love our stories and can easily get lost in them.

- Choose your examples carefully. If your example includes something exciting, like blood, that is all they will remember!

- If you call on a child to share, that child's contribution needs to be as explicit as your words would be. Make sure that student knows what he or she did and can articulate it clearly.

- Whenever possible, make your mini-lesson concrete. If you can use an analogy or a prop, do so. Give students something to hook on to when they are working independently.

- Your mini-lessons almost certainly won't address every single student, but they should address a need shared by at least 80 percent of the class. Small group and conferring will provide the scaffold for the other 20 percent.

- Use a familiar text as your mini-lesson literature model. As a class, choose a touchstone text that is familiar so that students can concentrate solely on the teaching point.

- Make sure your directions for independent work are crystal clear. Be specific about the choices for independent work: what to do, when to do it, and where to put it when it is complete. Remind students that no one is done until you say the workshop is over.

- Show, don't tell, during the teaching point. A demonstration through the form of a think-aloud or write-aloud should accompany every mini-lesson. Telling students to add details looks and sounds a lot different than showing them how to go back into a piece, find a confusing sentence, and add new details to help make the sentence more clear. Telling students to sound out a word doesn't mean a thing unless they are shown how to do it.

- Be a clown. Exaggerate and role-play behavior that you don't want to see. Students get a kick out of watching their teacher make a fool of herself! Making a point with humor goes a long way!

Mini-Lesson Format

Connection

We have been working on _____

_____

_____

Today I want to teach you how writers _____

_____

_____

Teaching Point

Let me show you how I _____

_____

_____

This will also help you as a reader because _____

_____

_____

Active Engagement

Turn to your partner and _____

_____

_____

Link to Future Work

So remember from now on to _____

_____

_____

Independent Practice

Although the mini-lesson portion of a workshop receives much attention, it is not the only part of the workshop. Students should spend most of the 45 minutes doing 'the work,' not listening to the teacher explain what work they will be doing. Independent practice is reserved for your students to try out the day's Target Skills in a way that is comfortable and meaningful for them. This time also provides another venue for you to re-teach, reinforce, or remediate as you confer with individual students or small groups. (There's more information about conferring on page 44.) Although we always hope students apply the teaching point of the day's lesson, it is all right if they approximate. They might not be developmentally ready quite yet or perhaps their topic doesn't lend itself to what you have taught. Continue to support these students by providing individual benchmarks identified through conferring.

Independent practice begins after you finish the mini-lesson. The purpose is to provide students time to practice, using materials that are supportive to their individual needs. In a reader's workshop, students will practice in their own basket of books that are just right for their independent reading level. During writer's workshops, students will be given choice of paper that is just right for their development. In writer's workshop, students engage in the writing process at their own stage of the process. Some students may be drafting while others may be editing. Although young writers generally begin a new piece each day, this does not have to be the case. A writers independent practice will fall where the writer left off the previous day. In a reader's workshop, students will engage in books selected weekly to support their growth as a reader. Books may include guided reading books, shared reading, or self-authored books. The point of independent practice in both areas of reading and writing is to allow students meaningful practice of the day's lesson with material that is not too difficult or too easy.

Because of teacher preference and class maturity, independent practice looks different in every classroom. Often independent practice is divided into sections to scaffold students as they gain fluency. For example, in one writer's workshop, the first ten minutes might be reserved for silent writing, where no one talks. Then when the timer goes off, students are allowed to converse with a partner or move about the room. Some teachers allow students to spend the last few minutes of workshop with their partners, engaging in targeted discussions about their work.

Independent practice is the time where students are practicing the work of being a writer and a reader, supported by you through the mini-lesson, a small group, or individual conference. Independent practice can be a good time to assist students in transferring knowledge gained in reading to problems they encounter in writing, and vice versa. For example, if the majority of the class is struggling with high frequency words during reader's workshop, then it would be most appropriate to have students spend the first five minutes of independent practice during writing workshop identifying high frequency words on the word wall and writing them quickly. This is why it is a good idea to hold reading and writing workshops back to back, and to confer with the same students on the same day: The reciprocity of the reading and writing processes becomes so clear to both teacher and students.

Conferring

While the class is engaged in independent practice, you should confer with students individually or in small groups. This is the time for explicit instruction directed at students you couldn't reach with your main lesson, or towards students with individual needs. These quick conversations give you a lot of bang for your instructional buck. When my youngest daughter was learning how to swim we missed the deadline for enrolling in group swimming lessons. I decided to enroll her in private lessons, even though they were more expensive and only 15 minutes long. But in just two of those sessions, Ande became a swimmer. The instructor focused on her, and the lessons were targeted at her specific needs. That is goal of conferring during the independent practice segment of writer's workshop.

Use the same mini-lesson structure for these conferences. Make a connection, explicitly state the teaching point with a demonstration, actively engage the student, and provide a link to ongoing work. This way of conferring provides a predictable structure for the student while scaffolding the conversation. Often, you can re-teach the day's mini-lesson almost verbatim, with additional individualized support for the student.

A typical conference falls into one of three areas: *content, strategy,* or *coaching.* During a content conference you might encourage the student to retell the story to make sure that she has the order of the story correct. A strategy conference might be directed towards how to segment words that the student doesn't recognize by sight. A coaching conference may remind the student to try a previously taught strategy that he is not using.

Each of the three conference types is effective, but a mix works best. Because it's easy to get into a rut, it's wise to record the type of conferences you have with each student. Many teachers often write in a compliment and suggest some next steps.

Teaching directly into what the students needs to move writing and reading forward is the essence of conferring. Students need to know that they have an audience who will become intimately involved with the work they are doing. Prepare for a conference through observing or research. Watch for an area of smart work to give a compliment, and for an entry point for your instruction.

If you have taught more than five minutes you know that a well-chosen compliment is the most effective way to motivate young children to repeat a positive behavior. By saying, "The way you used your picture to figure out this word was so smart. I want you to always do that because that is what smart readers do." Or, "The way you chose your words there was so smart because you helped your reader understand what you wanted to say." Make a huge deal when you see students using knowledge gained in writing to support their reading and vice versa.

Using your conference as an entry point for instruction is where the reading/writing connection can be most powerful. For example, if you are conferring with a young reader and notice during your research that he is not using one-to-one correspondence, you can lead the child to understand that one's spoken words can be represented by one group of words. Then during the writing conference you already know your entry point is going to be one-to-one matching. When the child is composing you can show him how saying a word slowly and writing down all the sounds will help him write the word. The whole idea that a blob of letters is really a spoken word is doubly supported through both conferences. You maximize your teaching opportunity by using what you know about a child as a reader to inform your point of instruction in writing, and vice versa. Students will repeat the behaviors that have been positively reinforced. We need to constantly be aware of this during both workshops.

On occasion during conferring or small group, you might notice particular students engaging in positive behaviors that should be shared with the entire class. When this occurs, take the time to make these children famous for their work. Stop the class and invite them to listen as you share the work of these particular children. After your announcement, challenge the rest of the class to think about incorporating this smart work into their own reading or writing. Although these interruptions are not really conferences, they do allow you to reinforce smart practice within the writing/reading community.

There are many professional books written around the art of conferring and ways to record helpful information during the conference. The bibliography on page 149 provides suggested titles for additional assistance in conferring.

The Teaching-Share

The last piece of the workshop is the *teaching-share*. This provides a time for the teacher to reinforce the work of the day, celebrate a student's reading or writing accomplishment, set the stage for new work to come, or to tackle a pesky behavior issue. The teaching-share provides the community with feedback—essential for nudging students forward in their literacy learning.

Since I wrote *Growing Up Writing*, I have changed the way I use the final sharing time at the end of the daily writer's workshop. I used to gather my students together and encourage three or four students to share their pieces, a favorite page, or a problem-solving word strategy. Then the audience would give the author feedback.

It seemed the children who begged to share every day loved this way of working. I was concerned, however, about the children who never wanted to share or who were not engaged during the sharing. Cathy Torres, a reading/writing staff developer in Pinellas County, addressed my concerns by modeling a new way of sharing. She helped me to treat the teaching-share as an opportunity to teach. With this type of sharing, I reflect on what has occurred during the workshop, or I spend time setting the stage for future work.

This new teaching-share is very effective. This final one to five minutes provides a time for you to reflect with the class about the day's work, highlight student work, set students up for a future teaching point, or dissolve a problem. This is not a time when students round-robin-read their work and stumble through an agonizing five minutes re-reading words with difficulty.

With this type of share, you usually function as the voice of the reflection, summarizing the work and what has happened during the workshop that day. It might sound like, "I want to share with you the smart work Tyra did today during workshop. She was writing a story about her trip to the beach. She wrote, 'I went to the beach. I went in the water. I looked for shells. I ate a hotdog. I went home.' But when Tyra and I talked, she realized that she really had three stories about the beach: going in the water, looking for shells, and eating the hotdogs. So when I asked her what her very favorite part of the day at the beach was, she said, 'Looking for shells.' So then she decided she was going to write a story just about looking for shells. Did you see how she did that? She re-read her story and realized she really had three stories, and now she is going to write just one. Tyra is learning to choose a *focus* for her story."

In reading, the teaching-share might sound like, "Corey was such a smart reader today. When he came to a tricky word, he looked for parts inside the word that he knew. The word was *store* and then he said, 'This part, *ore*, looks like my name.' Then he figured out the rest of the word. Nice work Corey, using what you know about a word to figure out a tricky word. I bet the rest of you readers could try that same thing tomorrow if you come to a tricky word."

Sometimes, however, you can use partner work as the structure for the teaching-share. Partners can talk about what work they did as writers that day, or they could read the favorite part of their piece together.

A teaching share can also set the class up for the next day's mini-lesson. To do this, you would restate the day's teaching point and end by showing a short piece you've written on the topic that you'll teach next time.

Finally, the share could be used to fix a problem they you noticed during the workshop. So the share could sound like, "Today I noticed that many writers were having trouble staying in their writing. They were looking around the room or talking to their neighbor. So tomorrow let's talk about some ways that would help you stay more into your writing." In this example, reading could easily be exchanged for writing!

My previous attempts at final share were wonderful for the child sitting in the author's chair receiving positive feedback from her peers. But now I am sure that the opportunity cost wasn't as great for the rest of the class. When you end workshop with one of these three types of teaching-shares, you control the share. You decide which writing or reading to highlight by what you want the class to go away with on that day. The final few minutes of writer's workshop present you with another opportunity to teach.

Much has been written about workshop teaching and the power of a mini-lesson, independent practice with conferring, and a share. It is wise to remember that one workshop may be framed by reading and the other may be framed by writing, but you are truly teaching reading and writing in both. When the support of the alternate process is there, students will become flexible enough to use it.

Creating Partnerships that Help You Link Writing and Reading

Establishing partnerships during the first few weeks of school is a must. Behavior and expectations for partners are usually the same for reading and writing. Many teachers assign partners by aligning reading levels, others allow students to simply turn and talk to the person they are sitting beside on the floor during the mini-lesson or at their table.

Most teachers, however, find it easier to assign partners. By using a t-chart and sticky notes, you can assign partners, and move them around as needed. Students simply look at the chart to find out who their partners are. You can use the same partner for both writing and reading—it doesn't really matter as long as the partnerships are working together.

Effective partnerships are essential for the active engagement portion of the mini-lesson. A partner shares the pre-writing work, gets thinking activated, and allows you to hear who might need clarification or re-teaching. Partners reflect with one another; they do not usually write together. Partners can help with revising pieces—they often provide insight that you didn't see. They can supply the immediate feedback needed when you just can't get to everyone.

Mini-lessons on how partners work and talk together are essential in the beginning. Some of the operational mini-lessons in this book will help you teach students how to be an effective partner during workshops.

Spend time during the first weeks of school establishing partnerships, and practice the rules of good partners. Be explicit with the expectations for talking and working with each other. Operational mini-lessons in Chapter 5 help you teach the art of partnership explicitly. Use active engagement to practice partnership work and highlight those partners who are exemplary.

Linking reading and writing during partnership work can be seamless. Use the conversational stems below to stimulate thinking strategies that are used in reading to support writing. Remind students that comprehension strategies should be considered as they write as well as when they read. Point out that they will want to make sure that they have determined importance in their own writing by providing just the right information for their reader—not too much unimportant information, but enough details to get the gist of the story. Emphasize that writing with active verbs plays an important part in helping their reader visualize, and that re-reading often to check for confusion is as essential for a writer as it is for a reader.

Conversational Stems to Link Writing and Reading

Activating Prior Knowledge

- Tell your partner some topics that you know a lot about.
- What kind of books have you read lately? Was there a character that was a lot like you?
- Who do you like to write for?
- What do you like to read?

Focus

- Tell your partner the most important part of your story.
- Tell your partner the most important part of your book.
- Have your partner tell you what he thinks is the most important part?

Elaboration

- Choose one place to tell your partner more than what is on the page.
- What do you think were the big ideas in this piece? In this book?

Monitoring for Meaning

- Before you begin writing today, turn and talk to your partner and retell the main things that have happened in your story so far.
- Before you begin reading today, review with your partner what has happened so far.
- Before you begin writing today, turn and tell your story across your hand.
- After you read today, tell the story to your partner across your hand.
- Go back and re-read your story and make sure that your reader will get your story so far. Check that out with your partner.
- Place a sticky note in your book, stop there and tell your partner the story so far.

Questioning

- Turn and ask your partner, "What else will my reader need to know?"
- Discuss with your partner what you think the author wanted you to think after you read this book.

Envisioning

- Read the first part of your story to your partner and let them tell you what they are seeing as you read.
- After you have each read this book, draw a picture together that shows what you were seeing as you read.
- Read your story to your partner, let them tell you what they are hearing, feeling, etc.

Accumulating the Text

- Turn and talk to your partner about what you will add to your piece today. Will that part make sense with what you written so far?
- Turn and tell your partner, "Ask what has happened so far in your book?" Does that fit with what you know about the story and the characters?
- Let your partner tell you the important part of the beginning of your story. Is that the part you want him to remember? Will that play an important part with the rest of your story?

Predicting

- Read the title of your piece and have your partner predict what might happen in your story.
- Read the title of the book and predict what the story might be inside.
- Talk together about how the text is put together. How does this help you know what might happen next?

Inferring

- Turn and talk to your partner about how you let your reader know how you were feeling without telling them.
- Turn and talk to your partner about how you let your reader know how what you were thinking without writing it.

Synthesizing

- Do you have a big theme in your piece?
- Discuss the theme of this book.

Spelling/Phonics

- Look at a tricky word with your partner. Say it slow, check the letter. Does it match the sound?
- Check with your partner to find the word on the word wall.
- Ask your partner, "Does this word look right? Does it sound right? Does it make sense?"

Partnerships can play a very important part in your workshop. With practice and high expectations, students can support each others' learning with determination and grace.

— CHAPTER FOUR —

Mini-Lessons that Support Writing and Reading

In *Growing Up Writing*, Sherra Jones and I identified four categories of writing mini-lessons: *Operational*, *Print Awareness*, *Foundational*, and *Craft*. I use them again here because I still find these helpful categories to ensure a balance in my K-2 writing instruction. Each category is identified by its instructional purpose, and together they address the unique needs of the K-2 writer. Each type provides an opportunity to connect reading and writing.

The mini-lessons included in the following chapters were written to be taught during writer's workshop, yet they all support reading skills and strategies as well. Teach them during writer's workshop, during small group, or as whole-group lessons. Pull from these lessons throughout the day. Where the target skill is appropriate, re-teach and reinforce it during any part of the day. Make the connection for your students often. The reciprocity of both literacy processes will assist your students as they become students who read as writers and write as readers.

Each chapter begins with a chart that identifies the teaching point and how it relates to reading and writing. The lessons follow the architecture of a mini-lesson, with the teaching point highlighted in bold print. Each lesson includes the explicit reading connection and an idea for a follow-through. Any prep work needed is noted at the beginning of each lesson. Although the lessons were written to be delivered in one sitting, there is no right or wrong way to teach the them. Many could be extended for remediation or extension. If a student is struggling with a particular literacy skill, perhaps re-teaching it through the alternate literacy process will support mastery.

You'll probably find yourself teaching operational mini-lessons more frequently at the beginning of the school year, but you should try to teach a variety of mini-lessons throughout the year. During the first month, try to resist your natural desire to move quickly ahead with print awareness, foundational, and craft lessons until you are sure that you've spent enough time making your students feel comfortable with the operational writing procedures. The operations you are teaching during writing will spill over to reading and hopefully make the day's instruction flow like a narrative.

You should expect K-2 students to take writing pieces through to publishing in a month's time. *Publishing* can mean anything from sharing a piece with a partner to reading it to a neighboring classroom. It could also mean inviting parents or members of the community in for a special event. Whatever form publishing takes from month to month, remember to teach the publication expectations explicitly during a mini-lesson. Celebrate the work done or students will quickly underestimate its value. Celebrations are the pats-on-the-back for a job well done. They cannot be dismissed as fluff. They are what keep our students coming back for more.

Operational Mini-Lessons

National Reading Panel research shows that young children work best in the classroom when given systematic instruction. Students simply do their best work in classrooms where processes are clearly defined. Operational mini-lessons provide basic, predictable information about the procedures and materials that K-2 students need to know and we need to follow for systematic teaching during writer's workshop. And although the materials used in writer's workshop may differ from those you would choose for reading workshop, many of the processes are the same for both. Many of the processes are the same for reading and writing workshops, so these can easily be taught together.

Operational mini-lessons lay the foundation for the entire school year. They allow orderly processes to be put in place so children can be responsible for their own learning within a reading and writing community. Transitioning to the gathering area, where to get paper, when to sharpen a pencil, how to work with a partner, etc., are basic techniques that children must learn. The mini-lesson format is perfect for defining procedures that will make these writing processes work. The workshop includes the children in the design of the workshop, which builds ownership in the writing community you are trying to build. The community's members learn the rules and how to follow them, behave respectfully, and offer support to each other. Operational mini-lessons help you create a safe community, which is essential for encouraging budding writers to take risks and move forward with their writing.

I use operational mini-lessons for teaching students the flow of the writer's workshop. Many of these operations are identical in both writing and reading, For example, teaching students how to talk about their learning with a partner is a vital skill for both reading and writing.

Note that there are no "right" or "wrong" procedures. You can set up your workshop to meet your needs. But you need to include lessons that will give your young writers a clear idea of how the workshop will work and let them know what's expected of them.

Print Awareness Mini-Lessons

Understanding the alphabetic principle is a basic skill common to reading and writing. Print awareness mini-lessons directly address—and are the foundation for—this important reading/writing connection. Deficits in early reading instruction leave students unable to use letter-sound correspondence, recognize onset and rime, or internalize spelling patterns so they can decode words fluently. Readers do not read fluently and they comprehend poorly when they lack the ability to attack words automatically. Writing gives students an ideal opportunity to practice word attack from the inside out.

You can use writer's workshop as a natural and important strategy to teach, re-teach, and practice these critical reading skills. Print awareness mini-lessons provide authentic practice for phonics and for all the other print strategies they are learning during reading.

Students will work their way through the phonics continuum beginning with mastering beginning and ending sounds. Teaching students to become flexible with letter/sound correspondence requires practice in decoding and encoding. As students learn the sounds that letters make in reading, they can also practice hearing the sounds the letters make and then recording those sounds. Teaching letter/sound correspondence by stretching out words, using digraphs, blends, and spelling patterns, putting spaces, punctuation and environmental print around the room are mini-lessons that fit nicely into writer's workshop—and they support reading.

You'll probably teach print awareness mini-lessons throughout the year, but I think you'll teach them more frequently during the first months of school. As students become more familiar and confident with print, the focus will shift. Remember that the skills and strategies you are teaching in reading can also be supported through writing. For example, the same conversational stems can be used during both workshops as a teaching point that functions to move a child forward to the next stage of reading and writing.

Foundational Mini-Lessons

Teachers know that writers read much differently than their non-writing peers. Foundational mini-lessons help you explicitly teach the connection between the reader and the writer. Young writers will learn how to think about, choose, sketch, label, and write the information they deem important when telling their stories. For example, the first lesson for becoming a good writer is to read widely and with the intent to discover what the author has done as a writer. The questions that readers ask of the authors they read should also be the questions they ask of themselves. These lessons help teachers find ways to bridge the two processes. Students who have been explicitly taught how to choose topics for reading and writing recognize the importance of reading like a writer and writing like a reader.

A young writer also needs to learn the various purposes and forms for writing. Understanding that a piece of text can be written in one of two ways—narrative or non-narrative—will inform their first writing experiments and help them understand and apply basic concepts, like *intent of story*. Foundational mini-lessons expose students to the many opportunities they have for writing both to explain and to entertain.

A well-organized physical text will facilitate reading comprehension. The more students know about how a text is organized, the easier it will be for them to make sense of it. Reading actually requires you to connect your thinking to an author's thinking. That's why how to structure their thinking is a big part of an author's thinking (Fountas and Pinnell, 2006).

Because foundational mini-lessons teach the writer, not the writing, these building-block lessons focus on teaching students that writing is organized, how to look at writing, and how to interact with the structure of narrative and expository. These lessons lay the framework for later work with specific craft Target Skills that will make their writing stronger. It also lays the foundation for prediction in reading.

Foundational mini-lessons should occur throughout the year.

Craft Mini-Lessons

The last chapter contains craft mini-lessons which teach the deliberate decisions that all writers make when creating pieces that are interesting to read. The word *craft* implies a special way of doing something.

Craft moves writing beyond basic proficiency. Teaching children how to make deliberate choices about the words they use should be integral to writing instruction and should begin in kindergarten. Marcia Freeman often writes about the value of craft to engage the reader and the need for writers to give their readers jobs to do. When a student notices a beautiful word or a repeating line, she is noticing craft. When she decides to hook the reader's interest or add a simile or color word, she is learning to play with words in the same meaningful way that all good writers do. Teaching students to notice the deliberate moves of an author they read and enjoy will pave the way for students to use these same moves in their own writing.

Getting inside a piece of writing and mucking about in an attempt to make it better is the essence of these mini-lessons. Showing young writers they have choices in the words and designs of their pieces will open up a new writing world. These are lessons of manipulation: moving and switching, crossing out, and adding on, are processes that occur a great deal during the revision process. You can teach these mini-lessons before the young writers begin a piece or during revision.

The lessons are interactive and diverse, and they directly link reading with writing. Touchstone texts used as models show students what beautifully crafted language sounds like when read aloud. Young writers learn to use craft techniques themselves—whether the use of a repeating line, strong verbs in a how-to piece, or the power of a simile.

By using a literature model, for example, you can show your students how to begin a piece with a question hook—just like the author did—and then allow them to practice that skill themselves. Or, after showing them how another author begins a piece with a sound, they might take a walk round the building to listen for sounds to add to their own pieces.

CHAPTER FIVE

Operational Mini-Lessons

Operational mini-lessons define writer's workshop and its procedures and lay the foundation for the entire writing year. These mini-lessons help students take responsibility for their own learning. **Using time wisely, re-reading to clarify, managing space**—these are all stepping stones necessary for your students' success as readers and writers. Reminding them that literacy skills are used throughout the entire day will help them understand the thread of instruction that runs across the day, the month, and the year.

The thirteen operational mini-lessons that follow begin to teach students that their tasks as writers and readers are reciprocal: The job of a writer is to support her reader. The job of a reader is to use the supports that the writer provides.

How Operational Writing Mini-Lessons Support Reading

Operational Writing Target Skills	Equivalent Reading Target Skills
Choosing just-right paper. See page 56.	Choosing just-right books.
Managing a writing folder. See page 58.	Managing a book basket.
Using a stapler for attaching one page written around a big idea to another page. See page 61.	Reading over several pages of connected text.
Practicing the behaviors necessary for becoming a good writing partner. See page 62.	Practicing the behaviors necessary for becoming a good reading partner.
Talking with a partner around a piece of writing. See page 63.	Talking with a partner around a book.
Making sure that anyone can read your writing. See page 65.	Using strategies in order to read someone else's writing.
Setting goals for your writing. See page 67.	Setting goals in reading.
Decisions for using writing time wisely. See page 69.	Decisions for using reading time wisely.
Re-reading a piece of writing to make sure that the writing looks right, sounds right, and makes sense. See page 71.	Re-reading a book to make sure that the reading looks right, sounds right, and makes sense.
Re-reading to ensure nothing has been left out. See page 73.	Re-reading to clarify or revise thinking.
Choosing a piece to publish. See page 75.	Determining the author's purpose for publishing.
Using an editing checklist to assist with the conventions of print. See page 76.	Understanding the role of conventions of print.
Adding a cover and an appropriate title. See page 79.	Using the cover and title to make predictions about the content of a book.

Choosing Your Just-Right Paper

Reading Connection: The procedure for choosing just-right paper for writing follows the same procedure for choosing just-right books in reading. Just-right books for emergent readers provide support for growing into longer texts. In writing, the paper is the scaffold for allowing students to compose longer stories. Both literacy processes require students to make informed decisions about appropriate materials—books or paper—for independent practice.

Materials:
- different types of paper (see pages 29-33)
- two read-aloud picture books using multiple size illustrations and various lines of print

Prep Step: Gather multiple types of paper. The paper choice for each student will be determined by the nature of each writer.

Connection

Make the connection that readers read books that are just right for them—they choose books that have a look or structure that they know they will be able to understand in order to comprehend the story. They read books that will help them grow as readers. Show students two different picture books that you've used previously during read-aloud. Point out the differences in the size of the illustrations and lines of print. Talk about how the look of each book is different. Share that authors do that intentionally. They choose a look that will work best for the story they are going to write.

Point out that in your classroom, finding the right look means using the right paper. Reinforce that writers choose paper that will help support the type of writing they are going to compose. They choose paper that will allow them to grow as writers and will help their reader understand and enjoy their writing. **Today I want to teach you how to choose your just-right paper for your own story.**

Teach

Orally share two different choices for types of stories that you might like to write. Make one very simple and the other a little longer. Some examples:

Story One
> One sunny day I went outside and I saw a ladybug.

Story Two
> One dark night I looked under my bed and there were two green eyes looking at me. I screamed and my cat ran out from under the bed.

Then role-play how you would choose just-right paper to write your story. Come to the conclusion that the paper with the big picture box and one line would probably be better for the ladybug story and the picture box with three lines would probably work better for the cat story. Explain how the paper should be just-right for each story and each writer. As writers build their writing muscles and begin to write more fluently, they can write longer stories with more lines.

Discuss how sketching their story first in the big box will help them remember how their story goes and what words they will want to write. Remind them that they should practice stretching out words and writing the sounds they hear, and that the big picture box gives them room to label their sketches.

Writing on just-right paper, paper that doesn't have too many lines or not enough lines, is just like reading in a just-right book, a book that isn't too easy or too hard.

Active Engagement

Orally share two more stories (make one short and simple, one slightly longer and more complex). Call them story number one and story number two. Display two different types of paper. Hold up the first type. Have each student hold up the number of fingers that indicates which story (story number one or story number two) it would be most appropriate for. Repeat this with the second piece of paper.

Link to Future Work

Share where you will be keeping the paper choices and allow students to think for a minute about their stories for the day. Ask them to think about the type of paper they should use to support their story—and themselves—as writers. Call students up row by row to choose their paper for the day before they go to their writing spots.

Follow Up

As students begin to fill up their lines, you can teach them how to staple a new page to continue the story or have them choose paper with more lines. Encourage students to sketch their story first before they begin adding words to any page. ●

Managing a Writing Folder

Reading Connection: Managing materials is important in all content areas. Keeping all books and important papers together requires a system. Teaching a system for storing on-going work in writing can lead to the use of the same system in reading, science, social studies, and math. Requiring students to make a conscious decision about work that is complete and work that needs more attention will serve them well as they grow as readers and writers.

Materials:
- a two-pocket folder for each student, with a sun on one pocket and a moon on the other (see page 59 for reproducible)
- one teacher's writing folder with meaningful pictures glued to the front
- two finished writing pieces and two unfinished pieces
- old magazines
- glue
- parent letter (see page 60), if desired

Prep Step: If desired, send copies of parent letter home a week before doing this lesson. Prepare folders for each student.

Connection

Remind students of all the writing work they have been doing during writer's workshop. Compliment the number of pieces they have completed. Then discuss how sometimes a piece doesn't get completed in one day, or even in two days. Share that writers find it helpful to have a special place to keep their writing work. **Today I want to teach you how to manage your writing folder because then you will always be able to find the piece you want to work on.**

Teach

Display four to five pieces of your own writing. (These should be written on student paper and resemble pieces your students might be writing. Two should be finished and two should be unfinished.) Explain that you got these pieces out of your writing folder, but that not all of them are finished. Read your four pieces. Discuss with the class that you know you will want to return to the two incomplete pieces and that you will need a way to remember which ones are not finished. Share that one way to do this is to use a special writing folder.

Show the inside of your folder. Point out the sun and the moon. Explain that the sunny side is for the pieces that are awake and are still being worked on, and the moon side is for pieces that are done and have gone to sleep. By putting their pieces on the correct side of their two-pocket folders, writers can easily find the pieces they are working on. Have the students watch as you put your pieces in the correct pocket.

Active Engagement

Give each student their own writing folder and all their former writing pieces. (Some teachers keep these pieces in a file folder until they introduce these writing folders.) Ask students to go through their pieces and decide which should go on the sunny side (awake) or the moon side (asleep). Circulate and assist. If you have partnerships established in your classroom, consider having students work together to decide if a piece is finished or if it still needs work.

Link to Future Work

Remind students that from now on they will be keeping their writing in these special folders, and that they will need to build the habit of sorting their pieces to the sun side or the moon side.

If you would like students to personalize their folders, send the parent letter home a week prior to this lesson. Have students use their photographs and special items to decorate the front and back of their folders and to color the sun and the moon. You could also supply photos from magazines for students to use. These decorations should represent the uniqueness of each student. As a bonus, seeing your students' prior knowledge and interests will be helpful when crafting your reading instruction.

Follow Up

After the lesson, have students leave their folders on their desks showing the moon and the sun side. Walk around and let everyone admire how many pieces are on each side.

At another time, have students share some of the treasures they glued on their folders. Encourage them to share why they chose those items for their writing folders. ●

Dear Parents,

This year, your child will be involved in the practice of becoming a writer. Every day, your child will write. He or she will write the stories of childhood: losing a tooth, visiting a relative, loving a family member or pet, lists of favorite people, places and things, lists of not so favorite people, places, and things. These stories will become a cherished remembrance of this special year.

Individual folders will be provided to organize your child's writing. In order to personalize these special folders I am asking that students bring in "treasures" (pictures, stamps, ribbon, etc.) that they can use to decorate their folders in order to personalize this special place for storing their daily writing. The items you send will be glued onto your child's writing folder as reminders of the personal stories your child can tell. These folders will be sent home on the last day of school and will hopefully be a place where your child holds a tiny piece of their childhood.

Thank you in advance for your help.

Sincerely,

Please send in treasures in a baggie by _____

Using a Writer's Tool

Reading Connection: Reading across several pages of connected text is an important goal in reading. Similarly, when students write across pages, they experience firsthand how one page relates to the next. Students will understand that the order of a story does matter. They will learn that staples ensure a story stays intact as it was written.

Materials:
- paper
- stapler

Prep Step: Gather enough staplers for each table/group. Prepare Writing Tool chart using information like that found at the bottom of this page.

Connection

Show students several little guided reading books that are four or more pages. Discuss how the author must have decided that her story needed more than one page and needed a way to clip all the pages together. Find the staple and show the class. Remind students that they too, have been working on their own stories and that sometimes their stories take more than one page. Show a student piece that is more than one page. Share that you have been stapling their pages as needed but today is the day that they learn to clip their own pages together. **Today I want to teach you how to use a special writer's tool, a stapler.**

Teach

Read a one-page story that you have started. Then think through how the next page will go and get a new sheet of paper. Share aloud what you are going to sketch and then write on the new sheet of paper. Model how to staple the new page onto the previous one. Then discuss how you should put just one staple up in the left-hand corner to hold your papers together.

Share your Writing Tool chart and walk the class through the steps of adding a page. Have students tell the steps for using the stapler across their hands, holding one finger up for each step: first, second, next, then, and finally.

Active Engagement

Have the class pretend they are going to add a page to a story. Together role-play how to grab a sheet of just-right paper, find the left corner, put the paper in the stapler, and push.

Link to Future Work

Show the class where the staplers will be kept and decide together who will be responsible for adding staples to the stapler. Remind the class again that it only takes one staple to hold a story together. Stress that real authors would never cover their stories in staples because their stories are too special and important.

Follow Up

Repeat this lesson to model how to use tape to add on to a story, how to get a sharpened pencil, where to get colored pencils, etc. Every time you introduce a new tool, spend time teaching how to use the tool and where it will be kept in the classroom. ●

Writing Tool Rules

Tool: Stapler
Rule: 1 staple, left corner
Why? To add paper to your story

Tool: Tape
Rule: 1 piece, 1 inch
Why? To add a line to your story

Using Behaviors of a Good Writing Partner

Reading Connection: The use of partnerships in all curriculum areas requires students to actively engage in the practice of a taught skill or strategy. Practicing the behaviors of good partnerships is the same whether in reading or writing. Students must be explicitly taught how to act as a partner to another student. The following lesson introduces appropriate partnership behavior during writing workshop, but this lesson could take place in reading workshop as well.

Materials: none

Prep Step: Assign partners ahead of time by using clothespins with students' names attached to a t-chart.

Connection

Remind students of times when they have worked together with another person. Next, discuss how working with a partner during writer's workshop will allow writers to get feedback and help each other to become stronger writers. **Today I am going to teach you how to be good writing partner.**

Teach

Define a good writing partner as a friend who helps us make our writing better. Share that a good writing partner is a serious job. It is not always easy to have someone look at our writing in order to help us make it better. Tell your students that you have been studying what good writing partners do, and this is what you have noticed about them:

1. They sit hip to hip.
2. They hold their writing between them.
3. They always talk nicely to their partners.
4. They listen to each other.
5. They take turns sharing their pieces.
6. They ask one question.

Active Engagement

Invite a student to join you as a writing partner. Model how to be a good writing partner by following the points above. Have your partner bring one piece and you share one piece. Ask the question, "Did my writing make sense?"

Afterwards, remind the students of what you did and what your partner did. Then brainstorm some other questions you could have asked your partner. For example:

- Will you add on to this story or start a new piece?
- What was the most important part of your story?
- Which part of your story do you like the best?

Divide the class into partnerships and have them practice sitting hip to hip, pretending to hold a piece of writing between them. Role-play how to practice the remaining points.

Link to Future Work

Send partnerships off to choose one piece from their writing folders to share. Count to five and have them find a spot in the room to sit to share their writing together. Determine that partner one will go first. Have partner two follow along with his finger as partner one reads. Then have them switch roles. A chart using the six points would be a great visual aid to help partnerships with this work.

Follow Up

Once partnerships have been established, you can use them for many things. Use partnerships to edit for punctuation or spelling, to help spell unknown words, or to practice re-reading. Partnerships can also be used during active engagement. Having students turn and talk about their writing plans for the day helps cement those plans in their minds. ●

Talking with a Partner

Reading Connection: The talk between students is the power behind any learning. Explicitly teaching students how to listen and then respond appropriately will enhance learning in any curriculum area. Talking with a partner requires that students engage in the practice, say something back, and then support their own thinking. Student talk takes any new learning deeper and spreads previous learning wider.

Materials:
- Anchor chart for partnership talk

Prep Step: Assign partners. Make anchor chart.

Connection

Have students sit beside their partners. Explain that one way that writers rehearse and revise their thinking is by talking with a partner. Remind students of the work done in the previous mini-lesson. **Today I want to teach you how partners can talk with each other to grow their thinking even further.**

Teach

Share the most important behavior of a writing partner is as a support. Partners support each other by listening and providing feedback that is helpful not hurtful. Share that one way to be a good listener is to lean in towards the person who is talking and look directly at them. Then the listener should respond in one of three ways, so that the person talking knows that their partner is listening. The three ways are

> I heard you say...
> I like the part where...
> Can you say more about...?

Review the different conversational stems and then, with a student as your partner, model what those stems might sound like in a partnership conversation.

Active Engagement

Invite the class to be your partner. Use the script below. Assign the class to play the role of partner two. Review the parts and then act is out as if it was a real conference.

After, have two students role-play in partnerships. Assign each student the part of partner one or partner two.

> Partner 1: This is a piece I am working on about flamingoes. Would you listen to hear if this part makes sense?
>
> Partner 2: (leans in to listen) Yes, I would be happy to.
>
> Partner 1: Flamingos are birds that live in warm places.
>
> Partner 2: I heard you say that flamingos live in warm places. Can you say more about that?
>
> Partner 1: They live in swamps away from people.
>
> Partner 2: Oh, I didn't know that.
>
> Partner 1: Should I put that in my story?
>
> Partner 2: I like that part, I think you should.
>
> Partner 1: I will. Thank you for your help.

Debrief the partnership activity. It might sound something like: Did you see how the partners worked together? They weren't mean and no one got mad. They helped each other. That is what partners do. Then did you hear how partner one said, "Thank you for your help"? It is always important to be polite to your partner.

Link to Future Work

Ask students to chose one piece from their writing folders and then to get with their partners. Encourage them to work together, sharing their pieces, and looking for places they might change in their writing. Remind partners to use a conversation stem and to say "thank you." After students have had time to work with their partners, provide some individual quiet writing time to do the changes suggested during their partnerships.

Follow Up

Remind students often of the responsibility of being a partner. Encourage the use of conversation stems. Model how these same stems could be used during any partnership work throughout the day. ●

Writing So That Someone Else Can Read Your Writing

Reading Connection: Students use conventions of print in order to read any text. They must use those same conventions—spacing, letter/sound correspondence, and proper number of letters—when writing. The use of spaces in writing supports the concept of one-to-one match in reading. Letter/sound correspondence is the basis for decoding and encoding while reading. Finally, the practice of listening for sounds and writing them versus looking at letters and saying the sounds will accelerate the automaticity of both.

Materials:
- Four mock student pieces written on student paper: two hard to read and two easy to read
- one teacher-written piece

Prep Step: Write four mock student stories. Write one teacher piece with one sentence that is hard to read.

Connection

Remind students of how important it is to always write in a way that anyone could read it even if they weren't there. Explain that there are reasons why some writing can be read and other can't. **Today I want to teach you how to write so that anyone will be able to read your story.**

Teach

Pretend that you have four pieces of writing by a student from a previous year. (Make sure one piece has a difficult-to-read spot.) Share that you are going to show the class each story and they are going to decide if they can read it. Hold each piece so the class can see it. If possible, put the stories on overheads or under a document camera.

Make a list of why some stories are easy to read and why some aren't. The reasons could include not enough spaces between the words, not enough letters to match the sounds, too large a space between letters or words, a picture that doesn't match the words, etc. Model with your own piece how writers must look at their pieces to decide if they've made them easy to read. For example:

Last summer I went to the water park. My favorite slide was the one with clq and lotsoftwistsandturns.

Model how to go back and re-read your piece and check for spaces. Then go back and check to make sure you have all the sounds you need for each word. Share those are two ways to check if a piece can be read: nice spaces and the correct number of letter sounds.

Active Engagement

Add on to your piece by adding a line that can't be read easily. Ask students to look at your piece and help you fix the unreadable part so that it could be read by anyone. A good way to do this would be have them turn and talk to their partners about what you should do. Listen in and then share with the class ideas for making the unreadable part readable. Fix your piece so that it can be read.

Link to Future Work

Remind students to always check their writing to make sure that anyone could read it. Review the two ways to make a piece of writing readable: spaces and letter sounds. Make a chart for students to refer back to. As students discover other ways to make their writing more readable you could add on to the chart. Use student examples (or make your own) to illustrate the chart. (See sample below.)

Follow Up

Several times a month, ask students to look through their folders and determine if their writing is readable. Remind students of things that make it easy for others to read their writing: correct spacing, enough letters to match sounds, picture match, and neatness. ●

Ways to Make Your Writing Easy to Read

*Leave spaces between your words.

*Write a letter for every sound you hear.

*Write from the left to the right.

*Write from the top to the bottom.

*Make your letters fit in the paper.

*Make your picture match the words.

Making Goals for Your Writing

Reading Connection: It is important for students to know the expectations for continual improvement. Setting goals and self-reflection are necessary for growth in both reading and writing. Students can align literacy goals in order to work smarter towards reaching those goals. For example, a reading goal of competently retelling a narrative can be supported by writing in the structure of a narrative.

Materials:
- Goal sheet for each student

Prep Step: None.

Connection

Begin this lesson with a story about a hypothetical child you know that wanted to learn how to ride his bike before his birthday. Elaborate about how he had a special person show him how to ride a bike and who helped him practice. Then everyday when he got home from school he practiced by himself. On the first day he decided he would try to ride down the driveway to the mailbox. Then on the second day he tried to get to the neighbor's house, and then he tried to get to the middle of the block. Explain how he kept setting goals and then practicing until he made his goal. When he made one goal, he set another goal. Finally, by his birthday he was riding his bike beautifully. He met his big goal!

Explain that writers do the same thing. They set goals all year long so they can see themselves growing as a writer. Then finally, by the end of the year, their writing muscles become very strong and they are writing much better than on the first day of school. Explain that a goal is like a stepping stone to get you where you really want to be. **Today I want to teach you how to set a goal for your writing so that you can be the best writer that you can be.**

Teach

Show each student the goal sheet found on page 68. Go over each section and think aloud about how you would fill it out. Share how each of them will be filling out a goal sheet, and how every month students will reflect on their progress towards the goals they set. Writers can then decide if they need a new goal or will keep working on the current one. Remind them of the work they are doing in reading and scaffold students in writing. Hand out the goal sheets and fill them out together step-by-step. Students who need extra help could finish one-on-one during a conference.

Active Engagement

Ask students to share individual goals with their writing partner or the person sitting next to them.

Link to Future Work

Remind students to think about their goals every day as they write. Encourage them to do their very best to reach their goals. Have students give a simple thumbs-up after each workshop if they worked towards their goal that particular day.

Follow Up

Share each student's writing goals with their parents. Celebrate approximations towards those goals periodically by highlighting the work of individual students. Remember to make every student famous at some point during the month. ●

Goals for Writing

Name _____

Places I plan to write:

_____

_____

Things I need to practice:

    * _____

    * _____

    * _____

I will read my writing to:

_____

_____

An author I would like to study:

Deciding What to Do When You Think You Are Done

Reading Connection: Expectations for the use of class time is essential in both reading and writing. Differentiating instruction requires students to use time spent in independent practice wisely. Students must be taught explicitly how to proceed from one task to another independent of the teacher.

Materials:
- Chart found on page 70

Prep Step: Prepare chart found on page 70.

Connection

Remind students that they will be writing every day during writer's workshop. They will also be writing the entire time building stamina. Explain that stamina is being able to do something for a long period of time. Explain also, that their job this school year is to build stamina as a writer. The only way to build stamina is to do something everyday and to grow stronger and stronger every day. Share that is almost like they are growing writing muscles. **Today I want to teach you what to do when you think you are done during writing workshop.**

Teach

Share that sometimes you start a piece of writing and finish it before writer's workshop is done. Pretend to finish writing a piece and then just sit there looking around the room. Then say, "But then I realized I wasn't building my writing muscles just sitting here doing nothing so I thought of some other things that I could do and I am going to share them with you. I could go back and re-read my piece and add on to the sketch. I could go back

and re-read and add some more labels, words or sentences. I could start a new piece." Share with the students that they could do those things too.

Active Engagement

Ask students to pretend that they have just finished a piece of writing. Then have them turn and tell their partners the three things they could do to build stamina and build their writing muscles. Share the chart found on page 70.

Link to Future Work

Tell students that you will be watching today for students who know what to do when they think they are done with their piece of writing.

Follow Up

Continually reinforce the importance of spending writing time writing! Make famous students who keep their nose down writing the entire time. Celebrate the number of minutes the class writes each day building until they are writing for 20-30 minutes independently. ●

When I Think I'm Done, I Can...

1. Reread my piece

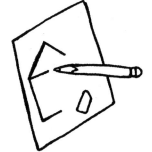

2. Add to the sketch

3. Add to the words

4. Start a new piece

Re-reading a Piece of Writing

Reading Connection: Encouraging the use of the different cueing systems in reading (visual, structural, and meaning) provides students with sources of information that aid comprehension. Ensuring that students apply those same sources of information when they write will assist them in writing to make meaning of their own text.

Materials:
- Story on page 72 written on chart paper
- Teacher piece of writing

Prep Step: Write the story from page 72 on chart paper or make a transparency. Write a story containing a problem area that doesn't look right, sound right, or make sense.

Connection

Share a scenario of a student (in another class, or from last year) that writes many, many stories. This student writes a story and then puts it away in his folder. Then he writes another story and puts it away in his folder. Share that he kept doing this day after day until one day his teacher said, "Today we are going to share a piece with a friend." So this little boy took one of his pieces out of his folder and he tried to read it but, bad news, it didn't make any sense. **Today I want to teach you how re-read your writing to make sure that it looks right, sounds right, and makes sense.**

Teach

Choose a piece of writing from your own writing folder. Make sure that you have spot where something doesn't sound right and doesn't make sense. Share that you are going to re-read your writing and if you hear something that doesn't sound right you are going to stop. Read the first few sentences until you get to your confusing part. Stop and say aloud, "Does this look right? Does this sound right? Does this make sense?" Answer appropriately, and then share aloud your plan for fixing your piece so that it looks right, sounds right, and makes sense.

Active Engagement

Allow the class to have a try at re-reading. Share the chart found on page 72. Choral read the paragraph. Together ask the questions, "Did this sound right? Does this look right? Did this make sense?" Because the answer is *no*, together go back and re-read until the point of confusion and discuss what could be fixed to make the piece sound right, look right, and make sense.

Link to Future Work

Remind students to always ask the questions of their own writing that they ask of the authors they read in class. Anytime during reading that something doesn't look right, sound right, or make sense, the text must be re-read to figure out the problem. Once the problem has been solved, the reader or writer can fix it.

Follow Up

Stop occasionally during writer's workshop and insist students go back and re-read their writing using the three sources of information. Verbally make the connection often during reading and writing: the text that you write must look right, sound right and make sense just as text that you read. ●

The Turtle

Yesterday on my way to school I saw a turtle crossing the road. He was sitting there green and it looked scared. On my way home.

The Turtle (fixed up)

Yesterday on my way to school I saw a turtle crossing the road. It was big and green and it looked scared just sitting there. I hope he is alright. I am going to look for him on my way home.

Re-reading to Check that Nothing Has Been Left Out

Reading Connection: As readers, students must re-read to clarify their thinking. If big holes of information are missing, a reader will struggle to make sense of the text. Re-reading is a helpful strategy for ensuring that information has not been missed. As writers, students must consciously include only the important information. Re-reading is the venue for ensuring nothing important has been excluded or that the story remains crystal clear.

Materials: None.

Prep Step: Write the two paragraphs found on page 74 on chart paper, or prepare a transparency.

Connection

Review the strategy of re-reading to make sure that you didn't miss any important information. Use an example of a familiar story or fairy tale. For example, you might say: Wouldn't it be a shame if I was reading "The Three Little Bears" but I wasn't really paying very close attention and I missed that part about the bears going out for a walk. I would have been confused through the entire story about why Goldilocks was in the bear's house and they didn't even know it. I would have to go back and re-read that story because it wouldn't have made sense. I would have to re-read to see if I missed some important information. The same thing is true when you are writing a story. It is always smart to re-read your writing to make sure that you didn't leave out any important information. You don't want your reader confused. **Today I want to teach you how to re-read your piece to make sure that nothing has been left out.**

Teach

Share the first paragraph found on page 74. Read it to the class. Ask for thumbs up if they felt confused, like something had been left out. Model how to re-read the paragraph to identify the place where information is missing. Identify the spot where the new information would go. Share the procedure:

1. Write.
2. Ask, "Did I leave anything out?"
3. Re-read.
4. Fix any spots where missing information should go.

Active Engagement

Share the second paragraph found on page 74. Read the paragraph together and ask if it sounds as if something is missing. Re-read to find the confusing spot and identify the place where new information could be added.

Link to Future Work

Remind students to always re-read their writing to make sure no important information has been left out. Share that writers, like readers, must always make meaning of the text in front of them. If the text doesn't make sense, re-read to look for the spot where the confusion begins and fix it!

Follow Up

Have students work in partners. One partner re-reads his piece while the other partner listens to make sure the story has no gaps where they story breaks down. ●

Paragraph One

Last fall I collected all the different colored leaves I could find. I wanted to them all over my table. I wonder if they will last.

Paragraph One (fixed up)

Last fall I collected all the different colored leaves I could find. I wanted to scatter them all over my table for decorations. I made a beautiful centerpiece of leaves and sat pumpkins in the middle. When fall was over, I packed them away for next year. I wonder if they will last.

Paragraph Two

One day I rode my bike to the park. It hurt so bad and it was bleeding. I cried all the way home.

Paragraph Two (fixed up)

One day I rode my bike to the park. When I turned onto the gravel road, my tire slipped and my bike fell over. I scrapped the skin off my knee on the gravel. It hurt so bad and it was bleeding. I cried all the way home.

Choosing a Piece to Publish

Reading Connection: Students will begin to notice that many of their favorite authors have published more than one book. Students need discussions about author choice. All authors have a purpose for writing and it is important for young writers to be conscious of the reasons authors have for publishing a piece.

Materials:
- teacher folder
- student pieces

Prep Step: Assemble four pieces to share with students and the chart of publishing criteria (optional).

Connection

Congratulate students on all of their hard writing work. Share that you know that writing can be exhausting at times but they have been persistent and worked hard at building their writing muscles. Remind students of a few of the books that you have been reading together. Share that all those books began as small pieces of writing just like theirs. Also share that published authors have possibly written many stories that readers doesn't know about. These authors had to make choices about which pieces to publish. **Today I want to teach you how to choose a writing piece to publish and share with others.**

Teach

Use your own writing folder to demonstrate how to choose an appropriate piece to publish. Have students watch as you examine four of your writing pieces. Make sure that two of the pieces are not complete and are not about any subject you really care about. Have two pieces that are complete, neat, have sketches, and are about something you are passionate about. Think aloud about the reasons why you like those pieces better (you might want to have these criteria on a chart):

- They are complete.
- They have a sketch.
- They are about a topic you really care about.
- You would like to share it with someone else.

Then choose the one that you feel is your very best work and declare that this will be the piece that you will publish to send out into the world.

Active Engagement

Have students return to their seats and go through their writing folders to pick out two pieces that they might want to publish. Remind them of the criteria. Ask them to return to the gathering area and sit beside their partners. Then have them decide with their partners which writing piece they will publish.

Link to Future Work

Collect their pieces to keep a follow-up lesson on editing.

Follow Up

Students will need to be taught how to edit for specific bottom-lines in their writing. Whatever editing skills you have taught (periods, capital letters, names on paper, etc.) should be used as criteria for editing a piece before publishing. Operational Mini-Lesson 12 provides a checklist and procedures for teaching students how to use an editing checklist. ●

Using an Editing Checklist

Reading Connection: Conventions of print make a written piece accessible to the reader. Students must know and understand that the basic conventions of print in reading in order to use them in writing.

Materials:
- editing checklist for each student
- class story on chart paper

Prep Step: Make sure every child has a piece to publish.

Connection

Remind students that they have learned how to choose a piece for publication. Discuss how the piece they have chosen is one they are proud of and love so much that they want it to be the very best! Explain that one way to check for excellence is to use a checklist to edit the words and punctuation marks used in the piece. **Today I want to teach you how to edit your piece by using a checklist.**

Teach

Explain that one way writers can fix up their writing is by using a checklist. Share that you have been looking closely at each student's writing and have noticed some *bumps*. These bumps are things like missing words, too many capital letters, or forgotten periods. Bumps are things that good writers know but sometimes forget. Checklists can help a writer make sure that there are no bumps that have to be smoothed out. Go over the checklists found on pages 77 and 78 and explain each area.

Use a class story on the easel to model how to use the checklist to find bumps and smooth them out. Then say, "Did you see how the checklist reminded me of things I forgot? Then I fixed those things. My piece is fixed up, it is smooth. Now it is your turn to try."

Active Engagement

There are examples of two different types of editing checklists found on pages 77 and 78. Whichever type you choose, remember to hold students accountable only for what you have taught them. If you haven't taught when to use a question mark, don't put it on the editing checklist. Consider adding photographs to each step to make it easier for younger students to read.

Hand out the pieces your students have chosen for publication and give them their own checklists. Have them edit their piece to smooth out any bumps. Then have them go over their piece again with their partners

Link to Future Work

Remind students that it is always important to re-read their writing to edit for bumps before publishing. Then when they publish their pieces and send them out to be enjoyed by others, they will be smooth and easier to read.

Follow Up

The next lesson should include adding a cover, a title, and color to their sketches. Change the editing checklist each month to include new conventions of print. ●

Editing Checklist

Name_____

◯ **I wrote my name on my piece.**

◯ **I read my writing.**

◯ **I stretched out my words.**

◯ **I left spaces between my words.**

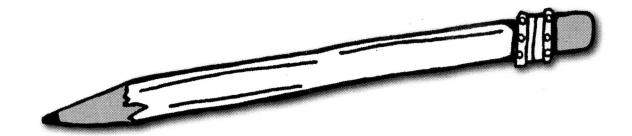

Editing Checklist

Name_____

○ I wrote my name on my piece.

○ I read my writing and asked myself.
   Do my words look right?
   Do my words sound right?
   Does my story make sense?

○ I have a capital letter at the
   beginning of each sentence.

○ I have a period at the end of each
   sentence.

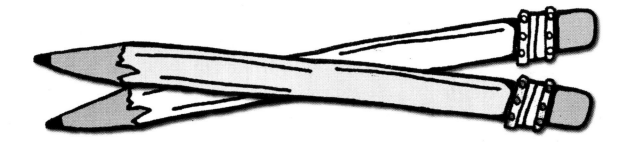

How to Add a Cover and a Title

Reading Connection: The first thing a reader uses to make a prediction about a book is the title and the cover. Covers come in multiple shapes and sizes and with various title fonts. Writers must ensure that the title and the cover of their books give enough information so that their reader has a hint to the story inside. The title and the cover is the first glimpse of the personality of the piece.

Materials:
- Construction paper
- Several teacher read-alouds
- Teacher piece

Prep Step: Cut construction-paper covers to fit story paper.

Connection

Read the cover and title of several books familiar to your students. Remind students that authors add a cover and a title to their books for two reasons: the cover holds the story together and the title and illustrations allow the reader to receive a hint about what is inside so they can start their thinking. The author gets to chose how to make his book look special and inviting so that others will want to read it. **Today I want to teach you how to add a cover and a title to your story so everyone will have a hint as to the story inside.**

Teach

Show the class one of your stories that is complete but has no cover or title. Read your story to the class and think aloud about some possible titles for your story. Allow them to hear why some titles wouldn't be appropriate. For example, if your story is about the pumpkin plant you grew from a seed, then the title shouldn't be "A Day at the Beach."

Decide on one title and then show the class where on the construction paper cover you could write the title. Look at your paper and make a decision about whether the cover should go horizontally or vertically. Then think aloud about some possible pictures you could add to the cover to help your reader know a little bit about the story inside.

Active Engagement

Have each student choose a sheet of construction paper. Make sure the fold for the cover is going the same way as the story. Then have them think about possible titles for their story. Remind them that the title should say something about the story inside. Then send them off to add an illustration. Circulate and staple the cover to the piece.

Link to Future Work

Remind students to always title the pieces that they chose to publish by adding a cover and an illustration that gives a hint to the story inside. ●

— CHAPTER SIX —
Print Awareness Mini-Lessons

Print awareness mini-lessons directly address the reading/writing connection. The ability to utilize the alphabetic principle requires students to have an understanding of the way print works. Students have many different experiences with letters and sounds. They must be exposed to how words work and what conventions of print allow writing to be accessible to the reader. Knowledge of the three sources of information, spelling, basic conventions, and spacing all are addressed in print awareness mini-lessons.

Literacy learning requires students to become flexible with print. With explicit teaching students can build on identified strengths. For example, students who know how to identify their name can use those known letters to begin to write the initial sounds as labels in their sketches. Students who can write the word, me can be taught to read the word me in connected text. As students gain more control over the alphabet the reciprocal nature of decoding and encoding can be reinforced within both reader's and writer's workshop. A student who can write the sentence, I like my Mom would certainly be able to read an emergent reader containing the pattern stem, I like... We take for granted that students see the connection between words they know how to write and words they know how to read. They don't. It is part of our responsibility as the teacher to continually bring those connections forward and teach into flexibility.

When we think about what students would need to know and be able to do with print to become a successful writer, it mirrors what students would need to know and be able to do to become a successful reader. In both forms of literacy we would want students to have accurate and rapid identification of the letters of the alphabet. We would want them to be consolidated in the alphabetic principle and understand and be able to use letter-sound correspondences, spelling patterns, syllables and identify word parts. Then we would want them to be able to apply all phonics elements while reading and writing. It just makes sense that we would teach these elements when it makes sense for the learner. If a student has more success with hearing a sound and recording the letter then recognizing a letter and matching the sound, then it might be more successful for that student to approach letter/sound correspondence through writing. We need to be as flexible with our teaching as we expect our students to be with encoding and decoding.

The following lessons are print awareness lessons that would assist students in moving up the phonics continuum. These lessons are written to be taught as a mini-lesson in writer's workshop but could be retaught in small group or conference during reader's workshop as well.

In *Phonics From A to Z*, Wiley Blevins gives these indicators of mastery of print awareness:

- Knows the difference between words and nonwords.
- Knows that print is print, no matter what form it appears.
- Knows that print can appear by itself or with pictures.
- Understands that print stands for speech, word by word.
- Understands the purpose of the space between words.
- Understands that words are read from left to right on a page.
- Understands that lines of text are read from top to bottom.
- Identifies the front of a book and a page in it.

The lessons in this section will support the acquisition of print awareness in both forms of literacy: reading and writing.

How Print-Awareness Writing Mini-Lessons Support Reading

Print-Awareness Target Skills	Equivalent Reading Target Skills
Stretching and writing words with approximation. See page 83.	Practicing letter/sound correspondence.
Writing with labels. See page 85.	Practicing letter/sound correspondence.
Checking to ensure all sounds have been recorded. See page 86.	Reading through entire words.
Using your finger to read your own writing. See page 88.	Tracking words in connected text.
Using known patterns in words to write unfamiliar words. See page 89.	Building a bank of familiar words.
Labeling with more interesting words. See page 90.	Increasing reading vocabulary.
Using a name chart as a resource in writing. See page 91.	Using a name chart as a resource in reading.
Using labels as anchor words in writing sentences. See page 93.	Finding anchor words when reading.
Writing words that you know fluently. See page 94.	Reading words that you can write fluently.
Leaving spaces between words. See page 95.	Supporting concept of word and one to one correspondence.
Writing from left-to-right and top-to-bottom on every page. See page 96.	Reading from left-to-right and top-to-bottom on every page.
Listening and recording sounds with a partner. See page 97.	Listening and reading books with a partner.
Re-reading in order to pay close attention to the meaning of all written words. See page 99.	Re-reading in order to pay close attention to the meaning of all words read.

Saying Words Slowly to Listen for Sounds

> **Reading Connection:** In reading, students practice decoding words by converting letters into sounds and blending them together to form words. In writing, students segment words into sounds for spelling. Encoding reinforces the learning of decoding. Both elements of phonics require students to practice the alphabetic principle.
>
> **Materials:**
> - sketch of a class shared experience
> - white boards and markers
>
> **Prep Step:** Prepare sketch. Enlarge word stretching chart.

Connection

Share that every writer in the room is learning how to become better at drawing sketches and writing words to tell their stories. However, explain that there are too many words in the world for them to be able to spell all of them correctly like in a book. So in order to write pieces using all the words they would need, they need a strategy. **Today I want to teach you how to stretch words out slowly and only write the letters that stand for the sounds that you hear.**

Teach

Have a sketch of a class shared experience story on a sheet of chart paper. Have some of the items labeled. Retell the class story using the sketch and explain that you have started to write some labels but there are some words you don't know how to spell. Point to a picture on the sketch and say the word that you don't know how to spell. Then explain that one way to write those words you don't know how to spell is to say them very slow, just like in slow motion, and listen for the sounds. Then you can write down the letters that you know stand for those sounds. Explain that even if you don't know all your letters you can write the ones you know until you learn more.

Choose another picture on the sketch and model again how to say the word slowly and listen for the sounds. Think aloud about how to choose which letter to write down for each sound. Then

run your finger under the word to check the word just as you would do in reading. Review again how you stretched the word slowly, listened for the sounds and recorded the letter that matches the sound. This process could become a chart that resembles the one found on page 84.

Active Engagement

Give each student a white board. Point to another picture on your sketch. Have the class say the word very slowly, like in slow motion, and record the first sound they hear on the white board. Ask them to hold their white boards up high so that you can see them. Reinforce correct letters and then write that letter under the picture on your sketch. Then ask students to say the word again, and record the next sound heard. Write that letter on the sketch. Complete this sequence until you have written all the sounds heard. It is not important that the word be spelled correctly but that students have recorded all the sounds. When the word is compete, insist that students run their finger underneath the word to check for sounds.

Link to Future Work

Remind students of the process they just practiced to stretch out a word and record the sounds with the correct letters. Go though each step again. If you are using the chart on the next page, go over it together. Encourage your students to always use this strategy whenever they need to write a word they don't know how to spell.

Follow Up

Many times students get hung up on only spelling words they know. Make a huge deal of any student who uses the stretching strategy to write unknown words. Share with your students often that they are just learning to write words and that it is all right not to spell every word correctly. Do not let them trap you into spelling words for them. If a student asks you how to spell a word, invite them to say the word slowly and then say, "What sounds did you hear? Write that down." ●

Say it S-l-o-w

1. Say the word s-l-o-w.

    s→n→a→i→l

2. Listen for the sound.

3. Write the letter that matches the sound.

    s n a l

4. Slide your finger under the word and check your letters.

Writing with Labels

Reading Connection: One- and two-word labels are the structure of most emergent story books. When students write in the genre they are reading, they learn its structure from the inside out. Labeling allows students application of the letter/sound relationship without the pressure of heavy comprehension work.

Materials:
- teacher sketch
- sticky notes
- pencils

Prep Step: Prepare the sketch described in the Connection section.

Connection

Show students a sketch you have drawn that includes you, a snake lying on the sidewalk, some flowers, a tree, and the sun. (Or you can use an illustration of your choice.) Share with the class that sketches play a very important part in telling a story but words have an important job too. Explain that writers often begin with a sketch and then label it by writing single words that go with each individual picture. **Today I am going to teach you how to write with labels because this will help your reader read the important parts of your sketch.**

Teach

Tell the story using your sketch by pointing to the appropriate parts: "One hot summer day I was walking up my sidewalk. I looked down and saw a snake. I screamed and ran the other way." Think aloud about which parts of your sketch you should put words—the labels—beside. Explain how you should label yourself in the sketch, the sidewalk, and definitely the snake. Share how some people might think it was caterpillar if you didn't label the drawing with the word, *snake*. You could even make a big O-shape with your mouth to show that you were screaming and put a speech bubble that says, "AHHHH!" Remind students to stretch the labels out slowly and write down the letters that stand for each sound that they hear. After you have labeled four to five items in your sketch, retell the story again, pointing to the words.

Active Engagement

Sketch a shared class story on chart paper. It could be a story about walking to lunch, a fire drill, etc. Make sure it is a story everyone knows. Retell the story together. Then give each student a sticky note and have them choose one item on the sketch and write a label for it. Invite each student to place their sticky note on the chart in the appropriate place when finished. Finally, retell the story pointing to the pictures and the labels. Explain that the labels help the reader understand the story by identifying the important parts of the sketch.

Link to Future Work

Remind students that authors write with pictures and words. Show students a few picture books that include both. Some great examples include: *Carlo Likes Reading* by Jessica Sanyol and *Cassie's Word Quilt* by Faith Ringgold.

Follow Up

Letter/sound correspondence can be practiced by writing labels for classroom objects. It can also be practiced during interactive writing groups, word work, shared reading, and independent reading. Give students the opportunity to label the bins in the classroom library, items around the room, or their desks. ●

Checking to Make Sure You Have Recorded All Your Sounds

Reading Connection: The relationship between sounds and their spelling is the basis of the alphabetic principle. Students must understand that words are made up of sounds and that those sounds are represented by letters. Practice in letter/sound correspondence while reading and writing will lead to automaticity in recognizing words encountered in text.

Materials:
- teacher piece on the easel, with labels underneath

Prep Step: Sketch one of your writing pieces on chart paper and add four to five labels. One label should only contain one sound. Prepare a simple sketch for each student.

Connection

Share that writers have a strategy for writing words they don't know how to spell: they say them out loud, slowly. This way they can listen for and record the letters that stand for those sounds.

Discuss how when writers don't put enough letters that stand for the sounds in the word, the reader won't be able to decode or figure out the word. It is the job of the writer to re-read every word and make sure they have recorded a letter for every sound that they hear in that word. **Today I want to teach you how to re-read your words to make sure that you have recorded all your sounds.**

Teach

On chart paper, share a sketch of two people playing with a round object. Pretend that it is your story (see example on page 87).

Think aloud as you try to remember if the story is about the time you were playing with a kite at the beach or if it was the story about making a snowman with your friend. Try to read the labels to help you. Demonstrate how hard it is to read them. Share with the class that there are not enough letters in the words to allow you to read

the labels. Explain that since you can't remember the story or read the labels, you are in trouble. You won't be able to continue the story.

Then show them how you could do things differently. Ask them to go back in time with you and pretend that you are just starting to work on your story. Share that it is the story of when you were playing with a kite in the sand at the beach. Have them watch how you re-read your labels several times by saying the word slowly, listening for the sounds in it and recording a letter for every sound. Discuss how once you have checked each word and recorded a letter for every sound, it will be easier for you to re-read your story.

Active Engagement

Give each student a copy of the same sketch. It could be a bird in a tree or a slide and a swing set. It doesn't matter what it is as long as it is simple. Invite students to label two or three pictures. Remind them to put their finger underneath each word, to say the word slowly, and to make sure that they have recorded all the sounds they hear. After a few minutes, stop them and ask them to get with their partners to check their work. They and their partners should be able to read the labels. This provides practice in encoding and then decoding text.

Link to Future Work

Remind students that this strategy needs to be practiced everyday. They must re-read their writing to make sure that every word they have written has a letter for every sound they hear. This way they—and their readers—will be able to decode their words and understand their stories.

Follow Up

This lesson will need to be repeated many times as students learn to stretch their words slowly and to record a letter for every sound they hear. Make the connection between decoding and encoding for your students. Share that during reading they are being given the letter and must find the sound. In writing it is simply the reverse, they must first think of the sound, and then record the letter. The process is the same; they are matching letters and sounds. ●

Using Your Finger to Read Your Writing

Reading Connection: Visually tracking words with the support of a finger allows students to check each word as it is read. Students must use the same strategy for tracking words whether reading connected text written by someone else or reading their own compositions.

Materials:
- sentences on chart paper

Prep Step: Write a few connected sentences on chart paper.

Connection

Ask students to close their eyes and picture how they look when they are reading. Have them turn and tell a partner what they imagine. Present the concept that there are behaviors that all readers share. One—used by both emergent readers *and* writers—is using a finger to track words as they are read. This keeps readers from losing track of where they are inside a word or in a sentence. **Today I want to teach you how to use your finger to track words in your own writing so you don't lose your place.**

Teach

Share the first sentence written on the chart. Ask students to watch you as you read the sentence. Point to each word as you read. Share how pointing to each word helps you to know if you forgot any words or read words that weren't there. Read the next sentence and include an extra word. Think aloud about how your finger didn't match each of the words. Go back and re-read slowly and use your finger to track the words. Remind the students of how you tracked with your finger.

Active Engagement

Give each student a sentence written on a strip of paper. Ask students to read the sentence with a partner. Take turns having each partner practice pointing under the words as they are read.

Link to Future Work

Remind students that using their fingers to track the words is as important to do with their own writing as it is in the books they are reading. Emphasize that this is a strategy they should use in both reading and writing.

Follow Up

Students who are reading independently at a level 8 running record will no longer need the strategy of finger tracking. These students should not need their fingers to track their own writing, either. However, students sometimes use their finger to mark a spot of confusion. Encourage this in both reading and writing. ●

Using Known Patterns to Write Unfamiliar Words

Reading Connection: Students who are ready to use analogies to decode and encode unfamiliar words will find strength in this strategy with both reading and writing. Noting similarities and differences between words will allow students to increase their known word bank by blending previously learned word parts. Paying attention to spelling patterns is necessary for students to store words in memory for use in reading and writing.

Materials:
- word wall
- chart paper
- white boards for each student (optional)

Prep Step: Identify words from the word wall that you will ask students to spell.

Connection

Remind students of previously learned words that are now displayed on the word wall. Re-read several of them together and reinforce how smart it is to know so many words. Discuss how there are thousands and thousands of words in the English language and that there is no way that they could possibly know how to read or spell of them. But there is a way to be able to read and write more words than are on the wall. **Today I want to teach you how to use the patterns in words you know to write unfamiliar words.**

Teach

Write a word from the word wall on the board or a sheet of chart paper. Read the word and underline the spelling pattern. Read the spelling pattern by blending the sounds together. Then say, "If I can spell _____, then I can spell _____. If I can read _____, then I can read _____" For example, if the word on the wall was *back*, you would say, "If I can spell <u>back</u>, then I can spell <u>sack</u>. If I can read <u>back</u>, then I can read <u>sack</u>." Continue writing words that have the same spelling pattern, modeling for students how

you use the same spelling pattern but change the beginning sound. Re-read the list of words that you made using the underlined spelling pattern.

Active Engagement

On a white board, have each student write an identified word off the word wall and underline the spelling pattern. Practice writing new words by adding new onsets to the familiar spelling pattern. Then choral read the words and then have students read their list to a partner.

Link to Future Work

Remind students that writers and readers always use the words they know to help them read and write.

Follow Up

This activity could be used to practice inflected endings or adding both onset and rime. It might sound like, "If I can spell *want*, then I can spell *wants*." Or "If I can spell *car* and I can spell *lap*, then I can spell *cap*." ●

Labeling with More Interesting Words

Reading Connection: Labels can provide practice in moving a piece away from the "right there" story and into inferring. One label, just one word, can change the entire feeling of a sketch or a complete piece. Encouraging the use of more sophisticated vocabulary builds a student's repertoire of known words. Students need practice using those important words.

Materials:
- teacher sketch

Prep Step: Prepare beach sketch on chart paper.

Connection

Remind students that labels are a way for readers to enjoy and understand the information in their sketch. Choosing just the right word to use as a label is important. Labels should be short, so they have to be chosen very carefully. **Today I want to teach you how to label your sketch with interesting words.**

Teach

Tell students that you are you are working on a story about going to the beach and getting a sunburn. Share a sketch that includes you, the sun, the beach, the water, the sand, etc. Think aloud about all the things you could label. Begin with the sun. Share with the class that anyone would probably be able to identify the sun in your sketch. However, most readers probably would not know how really, really hot it was that day. Think aloud about how you should label the picture of the sun. Decide to label it *hot, hot, hot* instead of simply, *sun.*

Model for students how to say the words of the label slowly, recording the letters to match each sound, and then re-reading to check. Go through this same scenario with the sketch of you. Share with the class how you didn't use enough sunscreen and got red. So beside the picture of you, make a label saying *sunburn* or *red.* Then you could add a speech bubble with the word, "ouch!" Remind students of how you thought about the

meaning behind your sketch, looked closely at the pictures and then thought of interesting words to use as labels. Discuss how students, when reading, should look closely at the pictures and then anticipate words they might find in the text.

Active Engagement

Remind students of the work you did by thinking about more interesting labels for the pictures in your sketch. Retell the story of your sunburn at the beach and ask students to help you think of a more interesting word for *water*. Have them share their ideas with their partners as you listen in. Discuss their ideas and choose one to add to your sketch. Some possibilities might include *ocean, wet, salty,* and *waves.*

Link to Future Work

Remind students that they should think about the meaning of their stories and use interesting labels. Discuss how labels can tell their readers something that they might not see in the story. While reading any book that contains labels, invite students to share ideas about why the author chose that particular label.

Follow Up

Assemble a class mural. Hang it in a literacy center and allow students to add their own labels. Use individual conferences to help specific students label with more interesting words. ●

Using a Name Chart as a Resource to Help You Spell

Reading Connection: Resources are essential tools for assisting students in becoming successful word solvers. Building on skills mastered, such as individual names, will provide a scaffold for teaching unfamiliar words. When resources are shared between reading and writing, they become even more valuable.

Materials:
- class name chart
- individual name charts with student pictures arranged like they were in a yearbook (see page 92 for a reproducible sample)

Prep Step: Run name chart for each student.

Connection

Do a quick review of the names of the students in the class. Discuss how the names of the students in the class can actually become a tool to help each of them spell new words. **Today I want to teach you how to use a friend's name on a name chart to help you with words you don't know how to spell.**

Teach

Draw a sketch and think out loud about a sentence to use as a label: "I want to write, 'I ate ice cream at the park' to go with the story in my sketch." Underneath your sketch write, *I* and then stop on the word *ate*. Say /a/ several times. "Hmm, I can't remember how to make an *a*. What do I know about an *a*? I know that April's name starts with that sound. Let me find her name on the name chart. There it is, *April*. Oh, yeah, that is what an *a* looks like. Now I can write my *a*." Write an *a* and finish the word *ate*. Remind the class of how you said the unknown word, listened for the first sound, thought about a person's name that starts with that sound, and then found that name on the name chart.

Active Engagement

Ask the class to help you finish the last word in your sentence. Write, *ice cream at the,* but stop at the word *park*. Give each student a name chart and ask them to find the name of a person that would help you write the word, *park*. (If you don't have a student whose name begins with *P*, choose another word to write.) Work through *park* together.

Link to Future Work

Share that each writer in the class can use their individual name charts if they get stuck on how to make the letter that stands for a sound in the word they are writing. Encourage students to keep their name charts in their writing folders. Also, display a large version in the classroom.

Follow Up

This lesson could be repeated using a regular alphabet chart instead. Always work through the use of any tool whole group before allowing students to use it independently. ●

Note: Thanks to Gail Ramsdell for her ideas on this writing resource.

Star Names

Using Labels as Anchor Words

Reading Connection: Teaching students to find anchor words in reading is a helpful strategy for supporting a one-to-one match. Teach students that the labels they use on a sketch will become anchor words as they write sentences to match their sketch and help tell their story.

Materials:
- teacher-made sketch

Prep Step: Choose a literature book with illustrations.

Connection

Remind students of the importance of looking at illustrations before reading. Illustrations will activate their prior knowledge and give them a hint as to what the writing might be about. You might say, "Readers look at a picture and then look at the words. This gets their brains warmed up and ready to read. Readers think about what the story might be about and then look for words that they know. These words are called *anchor words* because they help you keep your place when you are reading. Labels in your writing can do the same thing." **Today I want to teach you how using labels as anchor words will help you in your own writing.**

Teach

Show the teacher-made sketch and retell the story that goes with it. It would be best if it was a shared class experience. Together choose some pictures to label. Point out the labels that are the most important and could be used as anchor words. These are the words that should go in their sentences. Show students how you would write a sentence using a few of the anchor words. Underline the anchor words and re-read the sentence. Then model how the anchor words can help you if you forget what the sentence says or if you read the sentence incorrectly with too many words.

Active Engagement

Show a page of a familiar Big Book, but cover the text. Have labels already written on sticky notes and placed on the book. (Have students make the labels if you have time.) Read the labels to the class. Then, using the labels, have students generate a sentence that might be found in the text. Have students share their sentences orally with a partner. Listen in and choose a few to write on a sheet of chart paper. Uncover the text from the book and read it to the class. Compare how close they were to writing a sentence like the author's.

Link to Future Work

Remind students that labels are very important words and can be used to anchor the sentences that go with their sketch. Reiterate that they have already done the hard work of stretching these words out. Using them in a sentence is the next step.

Follow Up

The above Active Engagement can be used multiple times with different genres. Activating prior knowledge by identifying possible anchor words is a helpful strategy at multiple reading and writing levels. ●

Writing Words You Know Lickety-Split

Reading Connection: Developing written fluency with words will support student ability to read those same words with automaticity. Reinforcing known words in writing will assist students with those words when they are encountered in connected text.

Materials:
- teacher story
- white boards

Prep Step: Write a familiar story on chart paper.

Connection

Remind students of the strategy for writing unknown words: say it slowly by stretching the word; listen for sounds; and then record the letters that stand for each sound. Discuss how there will be some words that they already how to spell: they won't need to say those words slowly. **Today I want to teach you how you write some words lickety-split and some words slowly, like a snail.**

Teach

Remind students of a story that you have shared orally and have identified as a piece you are working on. Place the written text on a chart and re-read it. Discuss how the piece is not complete and think aloud about the next sentence in the piece. Then compose that sentence in the air. Finally, write the sentence in front of the class. Discuss which words you know lickety-split and which words you must say slowly since you are unsure of how to spell them.

For example, if you were writing a story about dropping your ice cream cone on the floor, you could compose this sentence orally, "The ice cream fell on the floor." Think aloud about how you can spell *the* and *ice* lickety-split since you already know those words. Then share that you don't know the word *cream* so you would have to stretch that word out slowly. Model how to do that and then quickly write out *fell on the*. Remind

students that since you know how to spell those words you don't have to stretch them out. Finish the sentence by stretching out *floor*. Reiterate that you don't know how to write *floor* lickety-split so you had to stretch it out slowly to hear the sounds in order to know which letters to write.

Active Engagement

Invite students to help you write the next sentence of your story. Pass out white boards so students can write along with you. Compose the next sentence, making sure there will be some words the class can write lickety-split and some they will have to stretch out.

Link to Future Work

Remind students that writers will know some words that they can write lickety-split but that others will have to be stretched out slowly. Then choose a word-wall word and ask them to spell it quickly with you while writing it in the air. After workshop, ask students to share some of the words they knew lickety-split and some words that had to be stretched slowly.

Follow Up

Continue to redirect student to words on the word wall often. Remind them that word-wall words are words they should not have to stretch slowly. It is also helpful to teach into analogies modeled in Print Awareness Lesson 5. ●

Leaving Spaces between Your Words

Reading Connection: Leaving white spaces between words while writing provides evidence that students have mastered the concepts of word and one-to-one correspondence during reading. Students who exhibit difficulties with one-to-one matching while reading will benefit from the instruction of using spaces during writing.

Materials:
- chart paper
- white boards and markers for each student
- bumper sticks (tongue depressors) for each student

Prep Step: On chart paper, write a line from a familiar poem or song. Do not put spaces between the words.

Connection

Remind students of the books they have enjoyed during shared reading. Using a Big Book, point out the spaces between the words and explain that these spaces help the reader know when one word stops and another begins. This helps the reader understand the story. **Today I want to teach you how to leave spaces between your words.**

Teach

Show students a sentence from a familiar poem or song where the words have been scrunched together. Invite students to try to read the sentence. Discuss how it is difficult to read because there are no spaces between the words. Share that when writers have stretched out a word, listened for the sounds, and written the letters for those sounds, he knows it is time for a space because there are no more letters to write. It is time to go on to the next word. Rewrite the sentence from the chart paper. Demonstrate how the bumper stick can help keep words from bumping into each other. Re-read the sentence, pointing out how much easier it is to read because the words are not bumping into each other.

Active Engagement

Give each student a bumper stick, white board, and marker. Together compose a sentence and write it word by word. After each word, direct students to use their bumper sticks to ensure their words have plenty of space between them. Remind students of how writers leave a space after they have written all the letters in a word. Re-read the sentence together. Point out the word-space-word-space pattern.

Link to Future Work

Remind students that they should always leave a space between words. The pattern of word, space, word, space, should be in every sentence. Discuss how scrunched up words make it too difficult to find the beginning and ending of a word and that makes it very hard to read.

Follow Up

Students who continue to experience difficulty with spaces can be brought together for small-group practice. After sharing the words in their sentences orally, make lines to match each spoken word so students can witness the word/space pattern. For example in, "I fell off my bike," you could make these lines:

_____ _____ _____

_____ _____. ●

Writing from Left-to-Right and Top-to-Bottom

Reading Connection: Knowing what to expect every time they approach a text will build confidence in young readers and writers. Basic concepts of print can be reinforced daily through reading and writing. These concepts remain the same whether in published text or self-authored text.

Materials:
- familiar Big Book
- chart paper
- marker

Prep Step: Make 'How to Use the Space on Your Paper' chart using text at the bottom of this page.

Connection

Use a familiar Big Book to show how the author has written her sentences from the left to the right, from the top to the bottom, and with letters that fit nicely on the page. Share that authors do this so their readers will be able to navigate through the print. It is just like a map, it helps the reader know where to go. **Today I want to teach you how to use the space on your paper the best way you can so that all your words will fit nicely on your paper.**

Teach

Ask students to watch as you write the first sentence of a story you are working on. Say the sentence aloud. Write with inappropriate lower- and upper-case letters, overly large spaces between words, and letters scattered all over the page. Then invite the class to examine your writing to see if it is hard to read. Decide together why it is difficult to read. Reveal your pre-made chart.

Correctly rewrite your sentence. Share aloud the decision you make about where to begin, the size of your letters and how the words should fit on your paper.

Active Engagement

Show students a piece of writing that doesn't use appropriate spacing. Have students turn and talk to their partners about how that author could make better choices about spacing. Remind the class to refer to the chart.

Link to Future Work

Encourage students to use the chart to check their writing for spacing. Have students pay close attention to the way the authors of the books they are reading use spacing.

Follow Up

Continue to use the bumper sticker to help students who need extra support for spacing. Continually reinforce the idea that each student in your room is an author and the expectation is to use the conventions of print just like the authors that they are reading. ●

How to Use the Space on Your Paper

1. Start your writing on the left side.
2. Leave spaghetti-thin spaces between your letters.
3. Leave bumper spaces between your words.
4. Start your sentence at the top of the page.

Listening For Sounds with a Partner

Reading Connection: Partnership work is a scaffold for students in reading and writing. Practicing ways partners can support each other in meaningful ways is helpful in all curriculum areas. Modeling how to help a partner without giving away the correct response will encourage students to do the same during any partnership work.

Materials:
- chart paper

Prep Step: Compose chart. Assign partners to assist each other stretch and record letter sounds.

Connection

Remind students of how they have all become brave spellers, stretching words out they don't know how to spell and listening for the sounds and writing the letters down. Share that sometimes it is helpful to work with a partner to spell unknown words. **Today I want to teach you how to stretch out your words and listen for sounds all the way to the end of the word with a partner.**

Teach

Begin by sharing a sentence that the entire class will write together. Pretend that the class is your partner. Share your sentence aloud. For example, "We are becoming the authors of our own lives." Share that you know some words lickety-split but some of the words you will have to stretch. Write a few words and then stop on a word that will have to be stretched. Invite the class to assist you in stretching out the word. It might sound like this: "You are going to be my partner and help me with this word. Partners don't give answers—they help their partners discover the answer on their own. So as my partner you might stretch the word out with me so I can see your mouth, or you might give me a word on the word wall that would help. Don't tell me the answer, give me support." Say the word that requires help aloud. Ask your partner (the class) to say it slowly with you. Pretend like that didn't help. Then ask your partner (the class) if there is a word on the word wall that could help you. Accept their suggestion and write the sound

that you hear. Continue to role-play to the end of the word, reinforcing that partners assist and help, they don't simply give answers.

Active Engagement

Involve the class in eliciting oral responses as to how a partner might assist in stretching out a word and listening for all of the sounds. Make a list that might look like this:

1. Say the word.
2. Stretch the word out together.
3. Find a helping word on the word wall.
4. Use the Name Chart.
5. Re-read the word together to check for all the sounds.
6. Ask you partner if the word looks right, sound right, and makes sense.

Link to Future Work

Remind students to use their partners to help them be brave spellers. Partnerships can provide the support to build confidence and engagement in practicing letter/sound correspondence.

Follow Up

Partnerships can be used in reading to help students decode unknown words by using the same chart developed in the active engagement. ●

Ways to Help Your Partner with a Word

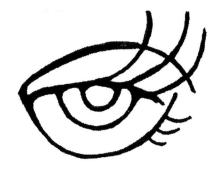

Look at the word wall.

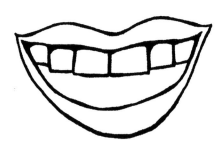

Say a word that sounds like your partner's word.

Fix This! Give a clue.

Re-reading to Ask Questions

Reading Connection: Students are taught three questions during reading instruction to assist in using fix-up strategies to monitor for comprehension. "Does it look right? Does it sound right? Does it make sense?" are stems students use to self-check their reading. Writers should use these same questions when re-reading their own work.

Materials:
- teacher-written story with some mistakes
- a story on chart paper
- Big Book

Prep Step: Write or glue a previous teacher story on chart paper. Write another very short story on chart paper. Prepare chart found on page 100.

Connection

Share with the class a familiar Big Book. Pretend like you know the author and share how she must have paid very close attention to the words because they all look right, sound right, and make sense. Share that this author knows that paying close attention to words will make a story easy to understand and enjoy. **Today I want to teach you how to re-read to ask yourself questions about your piece.**

Teach

Prepare a previously shared teacher-written story so that it is visible to all students. Include a few mistakes: leave out a word, forget to include an ending sound, or leave out a few letters. Re-read your story, pointing to each word and stopping every once and a while to ask yourself, "Does this look right? Does this sound right? Does this make sense?" Where the answer is *no*, fix the problem. After sharing your piece, asking the three questions, and fixing the problems, ask students to share what they noticed you did. Reiterate that writers must always re-read and then ask themselves, "Does this look right? Does this sound right? Does this make sense?" If the answer to any of those questions is *no*, they must fix the problem.

Active Engagement

Write the following two sentences on chart paper:

Yesterday a red bird was sitting in the tree in my yard.

It were stg on a nesting.

Ask students to read the first sentence aloud with you. Then have them turn to their partners and discuss together whether the sentence looked right, sounded right, and made sense. Then read the next sentence and have them work with their partners again to ask the three questions. Determine the problems with the second sentence and fix them together. Also determine whether this story sounds complete.

Link to Future Work

Share the Three Questions chart. Remind students that when they are writing or reading, these are three important questions to ask. Re-reading to fix problems is essential in both reading and writing. Remind students that understanding the story, whether reading it or writing it, is the ultimate goal.

Follow Up

Continue to emphasize the three cueing systems in writing as well as reading. Remind students that the purpose for writing their stories is to share them with others. Their readers will need to be able to make sense of their words. Besides the cueing system chart, encourage students to check themselves against the strategy chart found on page 101. This chart will provide reminders of the behaviors of strong writers. ●

Three Questions

say: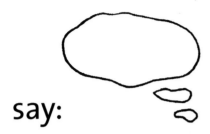

Do my words look right?

Do my words sound right?

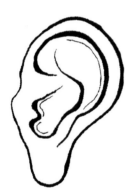

Do my words make sense?

Teaching Early Writing and Reading Together

Writing Strategies

Say your words s-l-o-w like a snail and listen for each sound.

Write a letter for every sound.

Write your words from left to right.

Put a bumper space between your words.

Think about how your story will go.

Touch the page and say how the story goes.

Sketch your story first.

Write with letters, words, and sentences.

One sunny day I jumped in the pool.

Re-read and ask yourself:

Does it <u>look</u> right?
Does it <u>sound</u> right?
Does it <u>make</u> sense?

— CHAPTER SEVEN —
Foundational Mini-Lessons

Foundational mini-lessons provide the support for all writing. There are basic rules of composition that must be followed in order for text to be understood. There are rules of language, organization, and genre. There is also the relationship between the illustration and the print. Students must be explicitly taught these foundations. When students are given strong building blocks, they will carry these strategies with them throughout every genre and stage of the writing process.

Identifying topics and fundamental organization of a piece are the basis for foundational mini-lessons. Students don't always realize that topics for writing swirl daily around their head. We must teach them to grab those pieces of their lives and write the story of that piece of time. We must show them how writing steps of a process will allow others to duplicate that process. Teaching others about a topic in which you are an expert is a very important type of writing and one that should be encouraged. Reminding students to keep their eyes wide open at all times to find that one tidbit for recording on paper is an important foundational lesson. Our students enjoy lives that are filled with stories and information, it is our job to help them stop long enough to let these topics land and grow.

Once our young writers find a topic, our next job is to teach them to envision their words within a structure. Identifying author's purpose will assist in the choice of structure and writers need to choose with intent. As students engage in wide reading across multiple genre, they will come to recognize the role organization plays in comprehending the text. Experimenting with a familiar topic in a new way, brings an excitement to the workshop.

Students will have the opportunity to study the structures of narrative and non-narrative text. They will practice writing in a list and label structure, non-fiction, how to and all about. The role of writing in the form of a diagram will be explored. Students are encouraged to read widely across multiple themes and genres. The same should be true in writing. Beginning writers need practice in composing in the structure of the text they are reading. Young writers will find comfort in predictable structures and come to realize that all topics can be framed in a way that works best for that particular type of writing. Using the scaffold of text structure will support both the practice of reading and writing.

As with all forms of writing and all types of text, re-reading to clarify meaning is essential. The practice of cross-checking for focus and clarity is taught comprehensively in reading. It should also be taught and reinforced in writing. As students experiment with different types of organizational patterns, they must be reminded to re-read though the eye of the person who will ultimately enjoy their piece. A structure that is haphazard and confusing will interfere with meaning. This is neither acceptable as a reader or a writer. This practice of re-reading in order to check for meaning is reciprocal and can be explicitly taught during both reader's and writer's workshop.

Foundational mini-lessons will require students to focus on basic organization of student-chosen topics. Once the topic and structure are identified, the words will come!

How Foundational Writing Mini-Lessons Support Reading

Foundational Writing Target Skills	Equivalent Reading Target Skills
Finding the stories of your life. See page 104.	Reading the stories that mirror your life.
Writing the stories of your life. See page 106.	Reading stories that support a text to self connection.
Drawing the entire story in your sketch. See page 108.	Using picture support in your reading.
Using pictures and words to tell a story. See page 110.	Using the illustration plus anchor words.
Planning a story across several pages. See page 111.	Accumulating the text.
Telling one small piece of a larger story. See page 112.	Realizing main idea with elaboration.
Writing with a partner. See page 113.	Reading with a partner.
Writing with a purpose. See page 114.	Reading with a purpose.
Writing within the structure of a list. See page 116.	Reading within a list structure.
Writing within the structure of expository. See page 119.	Reading a how-to text.
Writing within the structure of expository. See page 122.	Reading an all-about book.
Labeling a diagram. See page 124.	Reading a diagram.

Finding the Stories of Your Life

> **Reading Connection:** Prior knowledge supports reading comprehension. Leading students to realize that every single moment of their life adds to their repertoire of knowledge about the world is an important part of writing workshop. Stopping to take it all in, to remember what that moment looked liked, sounded like, felt like, etc., will emphasis the connections needed to comprehend text.
>
> **Materials:**
> - small paper bags or baggies
>
> **Prep Step:** Invite students to decorate little baggies with sequins or sparkles prior to this lesson.

Connection

Remind students of how their uniqueness defines who they are. Every student holds a special story that belongs only to them. Define *stories* as anything that happens to them. Every day, all day, stories happen. Encourage your students to look for them.

Share some personal examples of the stories of your life. Make them simple: discovering a bird nest, listening to it rain, or noticing a garden full of pretty flowers. Explain that the stories of your life don't have to be BIG events, like going Disney World. **Today I want to teach you how you can find the stories of your life.**

Teach

Tell the class they are going on trip to gather stories. Explain that they are going to take "magic story baggies" on a walk through the school and search for stories to gather. Tell them that when they see a story, they are going to catch it in their hands and put it in their baggie. Remind them that the story is invisible until is written, but that they will know it is there.

Give each student their decorated bag and take a walk. Whenever you see something that could be a story, point it out, and have students grab it in the air and put it in their bags. For example, stop outside and look at the clouds floating by or watch the workers around the school. Perhaps there is an anthill or a ladybug to watch or a bird in the tree. Allow students to take the time to stop and really look closely at their surroundings. After the walk, share some of the stories gathered. Remind

students that one of the ideas from their baggie could become their next story.

Note: if you would like your students to write one or two words, or make a sketch to remember their story idea you can use the baggie sheet on page 105.

Active Engagement

Invite students to pretend to go through their baggies and remember the stories they found on the walk. Have them turn and tell their partners their stories. Listen in and share some of the ideas with the group.

Link to Future Work

Remind students to always be on the lookout for a story. Share with them that a story can happen in the car, on the playground, in the lunchroom, or even on the sidewalk when lining up. Tell them that when they find a new story idea, they should catch it in their hand, put it in their pocket, and then add it to their baggies later.

Follow Up

Even as students begin to build stamina in writing, continue to remind them of the places authors get ideas for their stories. Before they go off to write, you can have them close their eyes and think back over the moments of previous days. Ask them to remember the stories they caught in their hands. Remind students of personal connections to the books that are read aloud throughout the day. These read alouds can become a springboard for writing individual stories during writer's workshop. ●

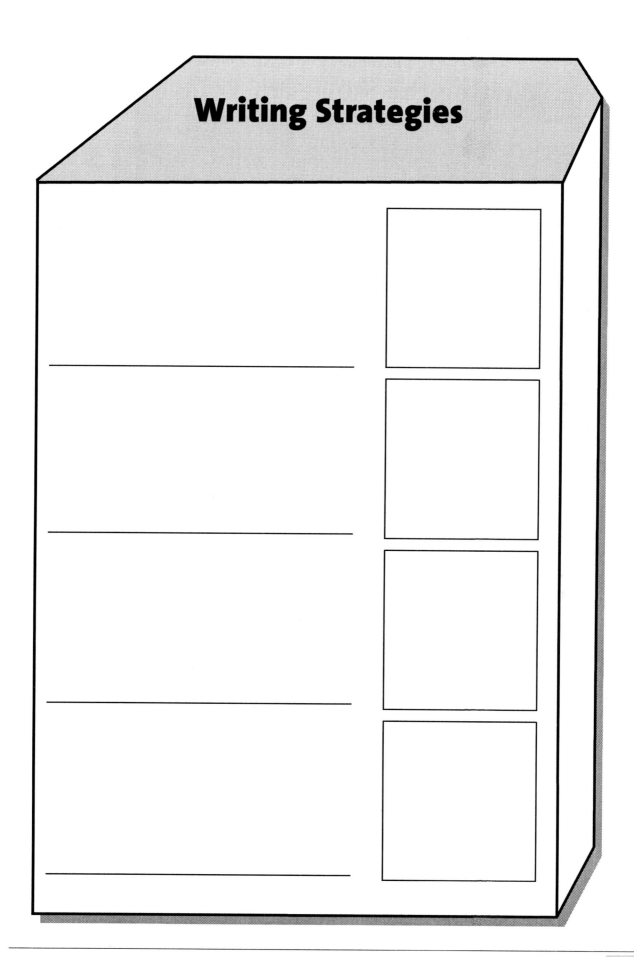

Writing Strategies

Writing the Stories of Your Life

Reading Connection: Readers make connections with events in which they have background knowledge. Calling student's attention to all they are exposed to in one day will help them find their connections. Young readers enjoy reading about children that are a lot like them. They read the stories of getting a new baby brother or sister, of dogs and cats, of planting a pumpkin seed or watching a cocoon change into a butterfly. These are the stories that students should write themselves.

Materials:
- recording sheet on page 107

Prep Step: Be prepared to share a story about a person you love, a place you like to go, and a thing you like to do.

Connection

Remind students of the work they have done catching stories in the air and keeping them in their baggies. They've been catching things they care about. Writers do the same thing: they write stories that they care about. **Today I want to teach you how to write the stories of your life.**

Teach

Share with the class the things that matter most to you. Share the names of a few people that you love, some places you like to go, and a few things you like to do. Then share a quick story about each. Explain that those are stories of your life and that they would make great writing topics. Thinking about the people you love, the places you like to go, and the things you like to do will help you find the stories of your life to write.

Active Engagement

Use the chart found on page 107 to review the three areas for story ideas. Then ask students to pick one area (people, place, or thing) to find a story from their life. Have students turn and talk to their partners about the topic they chose and then share their story orally. Listen in and share a few stories from each area.

Link to Future Work

Remind students they can always think about the people they love, places they like to go, or things they like to do to find a topic for writing.

Follow Up

Help students realize that they want to *tell* a story from one of the three areas, not just make a list. Remind students to focus on an event that happened with a person they love. Ask them to think back to what happened at their favorite place. Invite them to share the details of the things they like to do. Encourage students to begin their personal narratives with, *One day...* so that their topic takes on the form of a story. Share different structures for teaching someone else about an expert topic.

Examine class read-aloud books and discuss their topics and structures. Use these books as models for students to expert writing their topic in different ways. ●

Writing the Stories of Your Life

These are people I love.

These are places I like to go.

These are things I like to do.

Drawing the Entire Story in Your Sketch

Reading Connection: In most primary classrooms, the structure of choice is the picture book. The illustrations in most of these books hold much of the story. As students begin to understand the concept of story language, the illustration will hold most of the meaning. Sketching during writer's workshop will reinforce the importance of reading the illustrations in any book.

Materials:
- an illustration from a picture book or nursery rhyme
- chart paper
- marker

Prep Step: Choose an illustration from a picture book.

Connection

Congratulate students on how they have been finding and writing the stories of their lives. Share that writers first think about their story, then get a picture in their mind of how the story goes, and then put their whole story in their picture before they even begin to write words. **Today I want to teach you how to put your whole story in your picture.**

Teach

Show a picture from a familiar nursery rhyme or a page from a book with a detailed illustration. *My Little Island* by Frane' Lessac is a good choice. Cover up the words and think aloud about what you see happening in the picture. Reenact how the author must have thought first about how the story would go and then made a sketch. Share that the class should do the same thing. Begin with retelling a class shared experience: a fire drill, walking to lunch, someone losing a tooth, etc. Ask the class to watch as you put the class story into a sketch. Think aloud as you add important items to the sketch.

Active Engagement

Stop your sketching before you have included the whole story. Ask students to turn and talk to their partners about what else should be included in the sketch so the whole story is there. Listen in and share their ideas.

Link to Future Work

Remind students that they should follow these steps before they begin to write: Think about their story, plan what to include in the sketch, and then sketch the whole story. Share the chart found on page 109 as a reminder.

Follow Up

Remind students to include important items in their sketches so that the entire story is told. Teach them to retell the story using their sketch so that they will know if something important is left out. Have them read their sketches to their partners. Then those students who are ready to move on can begin to add labels to their sketches. Require students to sketch first so they will remember how their story will go.

Another way to reinforce this idea is to read aloud a page from a picture book. Hide the illustration from the class. Have students listen for the details and sketch what they see. Cross check the book's illustration. If the author has done a good job, there should be a close match. ●

How to Write a Story

Think about your story.

Touch the page and plan how the story will go.

Sketch your story across the pages.

Write letters, words, or sentences.

Using Pictures and Words to Tell Your Story

Reading Connection: Students are taught to use pictures as a strategy for making predictions about the text. They begin to expect that certain words portrayed in the illustration will be evident in the text. Connected text that students are reading use both pictures and words. Students should strive to use both in their stories as well.

Materials:
- sheet of writing paper for each student
- literature books

Prep Step: Collect literature books found in the bibliography (see page 147).

Connection

Compliment students for using sketches to tell their stories. Because young writers begin telling their stories through pictures it is important to nudge them towards using words when they write as well. **Today I want to teach you how writers use both pictures and words to tell their story.**

Teach

Begin by sharing some favorite picture books. Point out the place where the picture is and then the place where the words are. Suggestions for literature that explicitly show labels and sentences include *Carlo Loves Reading* by Jessica Spanyol, *School Bus* by Donald Crews, *In a People House* by Dr. Seuss, and *The Everything Book* by Denise Fleming. Explain that these authors told their stories through their pictures but then they also used labels and sentences.

Hold up a sheet of writing paper. Point to the place where you will draw your sketch and then to the place where you will write your words. The words could include labels embedded in the sketch or sentences below the picture box. Explain that your words will match the sketch in your story. Share a story quickly with your class and show them again where you will put the sketch and where you will put the words.

Active Engagement

Hand a sheet of paper to each student. Ask them to close their eyes and think about the story they will write today. Then have them turn to their partners and share their story. Then have them show their partners where the picture will go and where the words will go.

Link to Future Work

Remind the class how important it is to use pictures and words to tell their stories. Explain that you will be looking today to see writers using both.

Follow Up

It is important to remember that emergent writers will be approximating many of their words. That is fine. The purpose of this lesson is to nudge them to begin to use print, even if it is temporary spelling. Stop the class often during the next few workshops to celebrate students who are using words and pictures. Remind students that their words should match the pictures in their sketch. ●

Planning a Story across Pages

Reading Connection: Students must be able to hold the meaning of a story across several pages when they read. Accumulating the text requires students to sequence a story so that it makes sense. While writing a story, students must retell a story in a sequence that makes sense over several pages. Holding the meaning over several pages can be practiced in both reading and writing.

Materials:
- three-page booklets

Prep Step: Assemble a three-page booklet for every student by stapling together three sheets of paper of your choice.

Connection

Compliment students on the work they have been doing in telling and writing the stories of their lives. Discuss the importance of sketching before writing. Declare that you have noticed students elaborating more and more and encourage them to continue doing this. **Because your stories are growing, today I want to teach you how to plan your story across three pages, just like in a book.**

Teach

Share a simple story book with the class. It could be guided reading book or a picture book similar to *Night Whispers* by Angela Johnson. Show how the story goes across several pages. Explain that authors tell their stories across pages so they can elaborate or tell more. Also explain that writers must carefully plan each page out. Ask them to watch as you do this. Using a three-page booklet, tell a story from your life. Keep it simple. Touch the first page and say aloud how the story will go on that page. Then turn the page and share how that page will go before going on to the last page. It might sound something like this:

Page 1: Touch the sketch box and say: "I heard my cat meowing really, really loud so I looked out the window and saw him in the tree." (Turn the booklet page.)

Page 2: Touch the sketch box and say: "I went outside and yelled at him to come down." (Turn the booklet page.)

Page 3: Touch the sketch box and say: "He just looked at me and meowed. He wouldn't come down."

Remind the students of how you thought of your story, said it out loud, and then planned how it would go across the pages. Tell them that now you are ready to go back and sketch each page before adding words. Review the sequence: Think, Plan, Sketch, Write.

Active Engagement

Give each student a three-page booklet. Ask them to think about a story from their life. Encourage them to plan how the story will go by touching each page and saying how that page will go. Circulate and listen in as students practice this with their partners.

Link to Future Work

Remind your class that writing in booklets is a big step. Review how they should first think about their story, plan how it will go, and then sketch before adding any words. Call students who need extra support with three-page booklets into a small group for guided practice.

Follow Up

Continue to support students as they write in booklets. As students grow in proficiency, add pages as needed. ●

Telling One Small Piece of a Big Story

> **Reading Connection:** Tiny moments in time provide the depth of a story. When reading, students may accumulate those moments to infer and predict the outcome of the bigger story. Noticing the tiny actions and small details becomes more deliberate once students have been taught to write these in their own pieces.
>
> **Materials:**
> - three-page booklets
> - *Salt Hands* by Jane Chelsea Aragon (or any book with a small moment—see page 147)
>
> **Prep Step:** Assemble a three-page booklet for each student.

Connection

Compliment students on the writing work they have been doing—thinking, planning, sketching, labeling, etc. Share that today they are going to practice a writer's technique that will help their reader feel like they are right there in the story. **Today I am going to teach you how to tell just one small piece of your big story.**

Teach

Discuss how a story is like an orange. Talk about how a story is made up of small pieces, just like an orange is made up of slices. An orange slice is just one piece of the entire orange.

Read pages the first three pages of *Salt Hands* by Jane Chelsea Aragon. Explain that this is just a small piece of a big story: the author shared everything that happened in just that one moment when she went outside and the deer looked at her. It is like she wrote that moment in slow motion. She didn't include how she got ready for bed or how her bedroom looked. She concentrated on all the tiny actions and small details of only those few minutes.

Explain that sharing a small moment from a bigger story is something the class can try.

Active Engagement

Have the class watch as you walk slowly across the room and sit down in a chair, then pick up a book and pretend to read. Have students turn and talk with their partners about what they saw in that small moment. Give each student a three-page booklet. Encourage them to record that small moment of time across the pages. It might sound something like this:

Page One: The teacher walked slowly across the floor.

Page Two: Then she sat down carefully in the green chair.

Page Three: She picked a book from the basket, opened it slowly, and began to read.

Link to Future Work

Ask students to think about a small moment that has already happened that day at school. Give suggestions such as riding in the car to school, standing in the hall waiting for the bell, listening to announcements, etc. Have them choose one moment to plan across the pages of a three-page booklet. Encourage them to sketch and then write that moment. Remind them that remembering a story across pages is an important skill for writers and readers. It takes a lot of practice to get really good at it. Encourage the class to look for those small moments at home and at school.

Follow Up

Writing small moments will take much practice. Small moments are an introduction to *focus*. When conferring with students remind them to focus on the most important part of their story, that small moment in time. ●

Writing with a Partner

Reading Connection: Partners can assist each other in all content areas through the conversation between partners. Allowing students to ask for clarification or to provide support for their thinking enhances comprehension at all levels.

Materials:
- chart paper

Prep Step: Assign partners.

Connection

Share how working with a partner is a privilege and is a very important job. Partnerships are a way that members of the class can support each other. **Today I want to teach you how partners can support each other.**

Teach

Share the following chart about being a good writing partner. Go over each item and explain it fully.

How to Be a Good Writing Partner

1. Look at your partner when he is talking.
2. Take turns.
3. Say, "I don't understand. Can you tell me more?"
4. Can give a compliment by saying, "I like how you ..."

Choose a student to be your partner. Read one of your pieces to your partner. Then allow your partner to say either, "I don't understand, tell me more." or "I like how you..." Then change places and allow your partner to read her piece to you. Reiterate that this will be the process for working with partners.

Active Engagement

Allow students to join with their partners and read a previous piece. Partners should take turns and choose either question three or question four to ask their partners. Join back together to debrief partnership time. If needed, add other expectations to the chart.

Link to Future Work

Remind students that the job of working successfully with a partner is a basic foundation for becoming a good writer and reader. Part of the role of being a good partner is to support a fellow writer so that they can improve without hurting their feelings.

Follow Up

Provide positive reinforcement for partnerships that are working together successfully. Allow partnerships to remain in tact for reading and writing. ●

Writing with a Purpose

> **Reading Connection:** Good readers know how to ask questions and set their own purpose for reading. Deep comprehension is dependent on the reader's understanding of the text. In order to write a focused, understandable piece, students must be able to identify their purpose for writing before getting started. They also need to self-question throughout the piece to ensure that comprehension will not break down for their reader.
>
> **Materials:**
> - examples of different writing forms (card, recipe, story, invitation, etc.)
> - sticky notes
> - chart paper
>
> **Prep Step:** None.

Connection

Remind students of the many reasons that compel an author to write. Authors write to tell a story, to teach others how to do something, to invite others to a party, to give a compliment, or to remind someone to do something. Sometimes authors write down their feelings or they compose a letter. There are so many reasons to use print to communicate or inform. Remind students that they have practiced many of these ways all year. Remind them that now that they are authors of their own lives, they can choose when and why to use print to communicate or inform. **Today I want to teach you how write with a purpose.**

Teach

Discuss when you would need to use writing to communicate. Examples might include inviting someone to a party, reminding a family member of a dentist appointment, or reminding yourself to get milk at the grocery store. Explain that before you even began to write, you have to think of your purpose for writing. Remind the class that writers ask themselves, "Why am I writing this? What is my purpose?"

Share this example: If I were going to remind myself to buy milk at the grocery store, I wouldn't write myself an invitation to buy milk at the store—I would make a list. However, if I were going to write a story about a beautiful sunset, I wouldn't write it like a grocery list.

Explain that writers think first about the purpose of their piece. This helps them decide how the story will look and sound. Will it sound like a list or will it sound like an invitation? Will it sound like a story or will it sound like it is teaching something? Share that each writer must decide what form their writing should take. Hold up examples of different forms of writing and determine the author's purpose (i.e., recipe—to teach, story—to entertain, card—to acknowledge, note—to remind, magazine—to inform). Discuss how you knew just by looking at the form of the writing what purpose it would serve. Share that the author determined that purpose before even beginning to write.

Active Engagement

Ask students to think for a minute about what they will write today: a story, a card, a recipe? Have them think about the purpose and then turn and tell their partners. Then have them determine what form the writing will take and choose the appropriate type of paper.

Link to Future Work

Remind students that they will have the opportunity to write for many reasons all year long. Reiterate that before writing, authors think about their purpose and choose the form of writing that supports that purpose. Remind them again that you wouldn't write a recipe in the form of a card or an invitation in the form of a story. Allow students to write in any form that supports their message. Have multiple kinds of paper available.

Follow Up

A writing center is a perfect place to practice writing for real life. After you have taught the structure of friendly letter, invitation, etc., place the materials in a center so students can use the language of print in a real world situation.

During reading, discuss author's purpose and explicitly teach the forms of writing. Students can be taught to expect that certain forms can be read in specific ways to aid comprehension. ●

Writing in the Structure of a List

> **Reading Connection:** Predictable structures provide a scaffold for beginning readers and writers. They allow students to use their knowledge of text structure to support comprehension. Teaching students to write in the structure of a list will increase their success with reading list books.
>
> **Materials:**
> * picture books with a list pattern
>
> **Prep Step:** Identify characteristics of these types of books. Read several examples aloud before this lesson.

Connection

Students need to understand the concept of list books that identify a big topic and then give examples. List books can be written with labels, one or two words, or repeating lines. Gather several examples and read them aloud before this lesson. (Some suggestions can be found on page 147.) Make a chart listing what students notice. This chart might include

* List books use pictures and words.
* List books have a big idea with examples.
* List books can have a pattern.
* List books can have labels.
* List books can be short or long.
* The title of the list book should tell about the list.

Today I want to teach you how to write a list book.

Teach

Share that you are going to be writing a list book that contains a big idea with examples. Remind students of a read aloud that used repeating lines. Model how you would write a list book: Identify a big topic and choose four or five examples that would support it. For example, your big topic could be *Pets* and some examples might be *Dogs make good pets, Cats make good pets, Fish make good pets*, etc. (Ideas for list topics can be found on page 117.) Model with a sheet of list paper how you would sketch each of those animals in the box provided and then label the animal underneath the repeating line. Remind students how to add a page if they want to add onto their list.

Active Engagement

Invite children to think for a minute about a big topic they could turn into a list. Have them whisper it to their partners. Then ask them to quietly make a list across their fingers naming what each page in their list book might say. Listen in and share out a few ideas.

Link to Future Work

Remind students to re-read their list books to make sure they didn't include a page that doesn't go with their topic. Encourage them to add a title and cover. (See page 118 for sample pattern paper.)

Follow Up

Have list books available for reference during writer's workshop. (Many emergent-level books would be considered list books. See suggestions on page 147.) List books could become a focus over time depending on how in-depth you want to be with them. Have students be on the lookout for the different kinds of lists that they might see. Start a class chart of different patterns noticed in list books. It might look like this:

* Lists with one or two words.
* Lists with a repeating line.
* Lists with a question and answer.
* Lists with a twist at the end.

Show students different ways they can write about their topic in a list structure. ●

Making Your Own Lists

- words I love

- favorites

- zoo animals/farm animals

- things that are cold/hot

- things that swim in the sea

- family/friends

- things that can fly or slither or crawl

- things I love/don't love

- things that are important to me

- fruits/vegetables

- colors/shapes/number words

- things you would see at the beach

- things that have wings

- things that start with the letter __

- reptiles/fish/mammals/birds

- movies/books/songs

- places I like to go

Teaching Early Writing and Reading Together

Writing *How-to* Stories

Reading Connection: Because students are tested so heavily with expository text, it is advisable that practice expository writing. Studying the specific components of expository text and then writing within that structure will bring an added dimension to the understanding of the genre.

Materials:
- non-fiction directions on how to do something
- how-to paper

Prep Step: Read aloud non-fiction text containing how-to pages.

Connection

Remind students of the different types of texts they read throughout the day. Connect these types of text to the author's purpose. Review the non-fiction text that you have been reading and share discoveries noticed within the text. Some examples might include: pictures and captions, different styles of font, new vocabulary, transition words, compare and contrast, description, cause and effect, directions, diagrams. Explain that each of their discoveries are characteristic of non-fiction text, they are ways to teach the reader. Share that today they will be learning to write a very specific kind of non-fiction text that teaches the reader: a how-to book. Explain that a how-to book gives directions for how to do something just like directions in a game or steps in a recipe. **Today I want to teach you how to write a how-to book to teach your reader how to do something.**

Teach

Begin by thinking aloud about some activities that you know well enough to teach someone else how to do it. After three or four suggestions, choose one that would make the most sense and has steps. For example, a how-to book about my mom wouldn't work, but a how to book on how I made a cake with my mom would. Invite the class to watch closely as you say the steps aloud across your fingers. Point out how each step is very specific and builds on the step before. Remind students that it is important to say your steps in order and to not leave anything out. Show the

class a sheet of how-to paper (see page 121). Then go back to the paper and touch each box and repeat the steps. Show where you will sketch and where you will write the words.

Active Engagement

Invite students to choose three topics for a how-to book. Remind them this topic must be something that they know enough about that they can teach someone else. Have them turn and tell their partners. Listen in and share out some of the appropriate examples. Be prepared to keep students who are struggling with finding a topic with you to support their search.

After choosing their topic, give each student a sheet of how-to paper and allow them to practice touching each box and saying aloud how the directions will go or will we put it behind this lesson?

Link to Future Work

When students have a strong idea for how the steps for their how-to book will go, send them off to sketch and write the directions. Continue to monitor for dead-end topics and forgotten steps.

Follow Up

Some students will need extra support with choosing a topic. Sharing strong examples will assist them in choosing a topic that contains steps. If needed make something together and then make a class book containing the steps. Some suggestions would include: making a ball out of clay, dissolving salt in water, or drawing a heart. Although the how-to paper only has three boxes, students can staple as many pages as needed to complete their steps. You could also have student add a materials page to the front of their booklet as well. It is always fun to have partners exchange how-to books and then try to follow the directions. Check the bibliography at the back for how-to book read aloud suggestions. ●

How to Write a How-To Book

Step One: Choose a topic.

Step Two: Get a sheet of How-To paper.

Step Three: Think about how the steps would go.

Step Four: Touch the box and say how the step will go.

Step Five: Sketch the steps and say the words.

Step Six: Write the steps.

_____

1.

_____

_____

_____

2.

_____

_____

_____

3.

_____

_____

_____

Writing *All-about* Stories

Reading Connection: Categorizing information is one way students can make sense of the immense amount of information they must process everyday. Learning all about any subject requires the reader to investigate multiple arenas. When students write all-about books they witness how pieces of information can be organized. Writing a table of contents and creating diagrams will allow students to practice how to create and then use these features of non-fiction text.

Materials:
* Table of contents page found on page 123

Prep Step: None.

Connection

Discuss how knowing a great deal about something can make someone an expert. Ask students to brainstorm a list of topics that they know a great deal know about. Some suggestions might be *animals*, *sports*, or *foods*. Remind students that no one person is an expert at everything. Talk about how writing an all-about book allows you to share what you know with other people. Explain that many people learn about their favorite topics from reading about them in books. **Today I want to teach you how to write your own all-about book to teach another person about something you know.**

Teach

Explain that writers have to think carefully about a topic for an all-about book. Discuss how you have to consider whether you're an expert in your topic. You also have to consider whether it's a good study topic or not. You might say something like this: "I have been thinking about topics for my all-about book. I was thinking about my family as a topic. I know a million stories about my family, so it's a topic I know about. But then again, it really doesn't seem to make sense to teach other people all about my family. I can't really see my friends deciding to read a book that teaches them all about my mom or my sisters. But I can see them reading a book all about snakes or frogs or

firemen. I think any of those would make a more interesting topic.

"What do I know about? What could I teach other people about? Let's see, I know something about playing the piano, and horses, and what horses eat. (*You can use three topics of your own—just ensure that the last two go together.*) Let me think about playing the piano. How would the chapters for that book go? Chapter one could be what a piano looks like, and the next chapter could be how to play the piano, and then... I can't think of any other chapters. I guess the piano wouldn't be a very good topic because I can't think of anything else that I know about it.

"Let me try the horse topic. I could have a chapter on different kinds of horses and another on taking care of your horse. Then I could write about what horses eat as a chapter. Oh, and then I could have a chapter on how to ride a horse. I think this is a much better topic. I am glad I thought that through and tried on some different topics just like I try on different sweaters when I'm shopping for a sweater."

Remind students that they should choose a topic in which they have some information that they could share with others. Assigning students to read books around their topic before beginning to write the text for their own book will correlate *reading to learn* and *learning to read*.

Active Engagement

Invite students to turn and talk to their partners about topics that meet the all-about criteria (something I know enough about that I could teach others about it). Listen in and share some different topic ideas. Model how to choose one and determine possible chapter ideas.

Link to Future Work

Have students think about the topic ideas discussed with their partners and choose one to try on. Hand out a table of contents sheet (see sample below) to each student and have them list the topic of their study book and their chapter ideas.

Follow Up

Make sure students have chosen an appropriate topic for their book by checking their table of contents. The text of the book can be written on regular lined paper coupled with any other type of paper that would scaffold the understanding of their all-about book. Determine the criteria for the kind of information required within the all-about book. Then have students write interesting information around their chosen topic. Make sure the book includes a table of contents, pertinent information about the topic, a diagram, and any other pages that would teach others about their topic. (See Foundational Mini-Lesson 12 on page 124 for a lesson on diagrams.) ●

Topic for Study

Table of Contents

1. _____

_____

2. _____

_____

3. _____

_____

4. _____

_____

Writing and Labeling a Diagram

Reading Connection: The ability to read diagrams is an important component of visual literacy. Students encounter diagrams in both narrative and non-narrative text. Holding on to the information in the text while examining a diagram is a skill that requires repeated practice. Designing diagrams will assist students in determining information that is essential for reading diagrams encountered in connected text.

Materials:
- diagram paper
- 3-4 diagram samples from a literature book

Prep Step: None.

Connection

Discuss the different types of text students encounter everyday as readers and writers: personal stories, poems, cards, all-about books, diagrams, etc. Talk about how each type is important. Share that today they will be working on diagrams. **Today I want to teach you how to draw and label a diagram so that your reader can learn about your topic in a new way.**

Teach

Show students several labeled diagrams. Look closely at what is labeled. Think aloud about what the diagram teaches you. Examine how the diagram resembles the real thing. Make comparisons to the sketches they made earlier in the year. Share that one way a writer can teach their reader about a topic is to use a diagram with labels. Point out how the author names or labels the important parts of the diagram. These are the parts that the author wants the reader to pay attention to. Share some situations when an author might want to use a diagram in a story. Display the diagram paper (see page 125) and explain that this would be the type of paper to use for this type of writing.

Active Engagement

Ask students to think of a topic. Then have them think about a diagram that would help their reader

learn more about that topic. For example, if a writer was composing a book about dogs, she could put a diagram of a dog in her piece to show the reader the parts of a dog. Ask students to turn and tell their partners about a diagram they could use in a new piece or one they could add to a former piece. Listen in and share some of their ideas.

Link to Future Work

Remind students that when they are writing they should always consider their purpose for writing and then choose the type of paper that would support them. Show the diagram paper again and remind students if they are teaching parts of something, then they should use the diagram paper. Make sure students know how to access all the different types of paper.

Follow Up

Other types of paper that you might use in non-fiction writing might include a table of contents paper, a sheet of paper that is divided into picture boxes to allow for the illustration and labeling of different types of a particular topic (ex. different types of dogs), or a glossary page. Once all of these pages have been introduced students can write not only text to teach their reader something but include other types of pages as well. ●

Title of Diagram

Different Types of _____

— CHAPTER EIGHT —
Craft Mini-Lessons

Craft mini-lessons provide considerations for moving your students' writing beyond basic proficiency. In these lessons, students are taught to muck about inside their writing to find ways to craft their words in ways that elevate the text. As your K-2 writers build a foundation and begin using strategies to compose complete thoughts, it is time to consider integrating craft mini-lessons into your instructional strategies. Writers are taught that they have many choices and that they are the boss of their own writing. Craft lessons can be very empowering.

During craft lessons the class should be actively involved in doing something that will improve their writing. This improvement then becomes a strategy for all the pieces that follow. Wonderful craft lessons come from the study of mentor authors. There are so many incredible examples of exemplary writing in the books found in classrooms and school libraries—we need to take advantage of the words our students hear in literature every day. Mentor authors become invaluable when students are given time to really study their style, structure, and writing moves. Students can be shown how to identify an effective writing technique, name it, and then envision it in their own writing. Teaching students how to listen for strong verbs, enticing leads, and interesting dialogue are all lessons that can be taught through reading or writing. Once explicitly taught, students can apply their knowledge of verbs, leads, and dialogue in their own writing. This is the essence of reading like a writer and writing like a reader.

Craft lessons allow students to elevate their writing. Once a basic structure of a piece is identified, students can begin to mold and shape that writing through various writing strategies. Students can be dazzled by the revisions available to them. The realization that the authors that they read and love must also revise before they send their pieces off to be published is often eye-opening. Revision is a necessary piece of the writing process. Even our earliest writers can re-read with an eye for improvement. Spending time making a good piece of writing even better will encourage students to take pride in their own writing and appreciate accomplished writing when they see it.

Having fun with words is important for building and using vocabulary. Students will enjoy using repeating lines and structures from favorite read alouds in their own text. Borrowing the techniques of other authors is an effective exercise for beginning writers. Once students can hear a technique in the work of others, experiment with it in their own writing, and then witness the transformation of their writing from good to even better, they will never read through the same lens again.

There are so many examples of stellar craft in the children's literature available to teachers today. I have included just a few examples at the end of this section as suggestions for models not mentioned exclusively in a craft lesson. Know that any piece of children's literature can be used for a craft lesson. The reciprocal nature of reading text, identifying the writer's technique, and then giving it a go in your own writing, is the reading/writing connection at its purest level. Have fun with all the 'crafting' to come!

How Craft Writing Mini-Lessons Support Reading

Craft Writing Target Skills	Equivalent Reading Target Skills
Writing with more specific words. See page 129.	Building a vocabulary of more specific words.
Writing to show, not tell. See page 130.	Envisioning tiny actions and senses detail.
Writing with a simile. See page 131.	Using comparison to envision.
Writing with an ellipsis. See page 132.	Reading with anticipation.
Inserting a talk bubble. See page 134.	Considering the internal thinking of a character.
Writing with dialogue. See page 135.	Reading with prosody and intonation intended by the author.
Writing a variety of speaker tags. See page 136.	Reading with expression.
Including the inside and outside characteristics of a character. See page 137.	Bonding with all facets of a character.
Writing with detail. See page 139.	Reading for detail.
Writing with sound words. See page 140.	Recognizing ways a reader brings himself into a story.
Adding on to the middle of a piece. See page 141.	Determining importance.
Using strong verbs. See page 142.	Reading to visualize the action.
Using patterns to create a mood. See page 143.	Repeating lines of text is purposeful.
Studying an author you love. See page 144.	Celebrating the deliberate intentions of authors you respect.

Writing with More Specific Words

Reading Connection: Teaching and developing vocabulary presents many challenges in all academic areas. Assessing the use of specific vocabulary in student writing is an effective way to bring words to life in a meaningful context. Students who know words but use them in vague or broad terms will benefit from explicit instruction in writing that will, in turn, spill over into their reading.

Materials:
- paint chip samples from a store that sells paint
- *Alexander and the Terrible, Horrible, No Good, Very Bad Day* by Judith Viorst

Prep Step: Write the list of fuzzy words on chart paper, collect enough paint chips strips for each student.

Connection

Show a list of words that are constant in student writing but not very powerful. These would be words such as *nice, good, fun, bad, went,* or *sad*. Explain that you have noticed these words appearing in student writing often. Then share that those words are really not very exciting words because they are fuzzy. They don't paint much of a picture. These words are not specific. **Today I want to teach you how to write with more specific words so that your stories will be crystal clear in the mind of your reader.**

Teach

Show the cover of Judith Viorst's book, *Alexander and the Terrible, Horrible, No Good, Very Bad Day.* Explain that Judith used many specific words in her title. From the beginning it was clear that Alexander's day wasn't just bad, it was more than bad. Judith painted a clear picture for her reader.

Use a paint-chip strip from any local store that sells paint. Using the examples from Viorst's book, write a synonym for *bad* on each shade of one color selection. Explain that just like a painter, writers use shades of words. But, also like a painter, it is important to use just the right shade of the right word. Share some quick scenarios

for each word. For example, if your dog ran away that would be *horrible*, if your sister broke your favorite toy that would be *terrible*, if your dad ate the last popsicle that would be *no good*, and if you lost your homework that would be *very bad*. Remind students that they each have to think very hard about specific words when they are composing to help their reader be completely clear in interpreting their piece.

Active Engagement

Hand out paint-chip strips to each student. Have them work in partners to choose a fuzzy word from the above connection and write different shades of the word. Share out specific words.

Link to Future Work

Remind students to always use specific words when writing. Remind them that more specific words paint a clearer picture for their reader.

Follow Up

Provide paint-chip strips in the writing center for students to make their own specific word tool to keep in their writing folder. Placing more specific words on a continuum is another venue for helping students to visualize more specific word choice. ●

Writing to Show, Not Tell

Reading Connection: Envisioning requires students to use their five senses to picture a scene while reading. While writing, students must incorporate these same senses to provide the information necessary to bring their story alive.

Materials:
- chart paper
- marker

Prep Step: None.

Connection

Remind students that every writer strives to paint a detailed picture with words. These words should allow the reader to make a movie in their mind. Remind students that a writer must use tiny actions to provide that level of detail about what is happening and how the characters are feeling. **Today I want to show you how to show—not tell—by using tiny actions because this will bring your story to life for your reader.**

Teach

At the top of a sheet of chart paper, write "I felt so happy." Ask students to be researchers and watch you closely for the tiny actions that prove that you feel happy. Jump in the air, smile broadly, pump your fists, and yell, "whoopee!" Then ask the class to name the actions they saw. Write these on chart paper. Re-read them to the class. Share that these tiny actions paint a much better picture than simply writing "I felt so happy." It is the tiny actions that show the reader what you were feeling.

Active Engagement

Provide different scenarios for the class to practice recording tiny actions. Some examples: *I felt so angry. I felt so sad. I felt so silly.* You could do this in whole groups or have partners work together.

Link to Future Work

Remind students to always think about the tiny actions that will make their story come alive. Say, "Remember to show, not tell, by writing all the tiny actions."

Follow Up

This lesson will need to be repeated many times before students can write with tiny actions consistently. Anytime you see this done well in a piece of literature, call your students' attention to the example of showing, not telling, using tiny actions. ●

Writing with a Simile

Reading Connection: Comparisons are one way that we all make sense of our world. Authors use comparisons to tell their readers what things look like, how they feel, etc. The use of similes is an effective strategy for reinforcing observational skills and logical thinking.

Materials:
- *Quick as a Cricket* by Audrey Wood or any other book with similes
- one small object (such as a marshmallow) for each partnership

Prep Step: Find something small enough for each partnership to examine and that lends itself to being compared to something obvious.

Connection

Remind students of the work they have been doing with showing, not telling. Explain that sometimes a writer can help the reader picture a moment or an item in their minds by comparing it to something familiar. **Today, I want to teach you how writers use similes to paint pictures with words.** *Similes* **are comparisons between two things using the words** *like* **or** *as***. Similes help your reader connect what they know to what you are telling them with your words.**

Teach

Use a picture book that contains several similes (*Quick as a Cricket* by Audrey Wood works well). Share that the main character, a little boy, compares himself to many things throughout the book so that we can get to know him. Read some of these similes aloud. You might say: "Did you see how the little boy compared himself to a cricket because a cricket is quick and so is he. Then he compared himself to an ant because an ant is small and so is he. Audrey Wood used similes, comparing two things using the word *as*, to help us picture the little boy. She thought about things the boy liked to do or how he felt and then thought about something she could compare the boy to that would paint the picture that she wanted us to

see." Explain that writing with comparisons is an effective way to write descriptively.

Active Engagement

Give each partnership the same small object, such a marshmallow. Ask partners to work together to compare the marshmallow to something else. Have them think about how they want their reader to see the marshmallow: what does it look like, feel like, taste like, etc. Then think about what you could compare it to using the words like or as. Listen in to their ideas. Share out a few. Then record some of them on chart paper (*as fluffy as a cloud, as white as snow, as soft as cotton,* etc.)

Link to Future Work

Remind students that anytime they need to paint pictures in their reader's mind, they can use similes. Remind them that similes are comparisons between two things using the words *as* or *like*, and that they allow reader to see exactly what the writer is seeing.

Follow Up

There are many picture books that provide models for similes. Keep a class chart of the similes students notice while reading. ●

Writing with an Ellipsis

Reading Connection: Punctuation allows text to be read as the writer intended. Teaching students the purpose of punctuation marks in writing will enhance fluency and encourage prosody in reading. Once students learn the function of an ellipse in either reading or writing, they can use it with flexibility between processes.

Materials:
- teacher- or class-shared story
- book with an ellipsis
- chart paper
- story for active engagement

Prep Step: Run off story for active engagement. Write story on chart.

Connection

Share with the class that they have been studying and thinking about punctuation they could try in their own writing. One place to look for different types of punctuation is in books. Remind them that it is always smart to notice what other authors do. **Today I want to teach you how to use an *ellipsis*, a special kind of punctuation that encourages your reader to pause at appropriate places in your story.**

Teach

Share a page of book that contains an ellipsis. (Ezra Jack Keats is an author who uses ellipses often.) Ask students to notice the punctuation. Explain that an ellipsis is three dots that are used whenever an author wants to slow his reader down and make them think about what might happen next. Re-read your example from the book again so the class can hear how this sounds.

Use a previous story—either one of yours or an oral class story—to model how to add an ellipsis to slow the reader down. Make sure the story is on chart paper so everyone can see your work. Think aloud about where you would want to slow your reader down in order to create some suspense and then add the ellipsis.

Active Engagement

Provide each student with a copy of the story found on page 133. Have students work together to find a place in the story that could effectively use an ellipses to slow the reader down. Share class discussions about where the ellipsis should go.

Link to Future Work

Remind students that an ellipsis can be used anytime they want to slow their reader down and anticipate what might come next.

Follow Up

Invite students to be on the lookout for ellipses in the books they are reading and in the picture books you read aloud. Students who embrace ellipses might enjoy giving the dash or hyphen a try as well. If *ellipsis* is too hard a word to remember, decide together what to call this type of punctuation (such as the *dot dot dot*). Naming the feature in a way that students will remember and use is more important than remembering the specific word. ●

My grandma was coming to visit. We went to the bus station to pick her up. I waited and waited and waited. Finally, she came off the bus and I ran to give her a big hug.

Inserting a Talk Bubble

Reading Connection: Thinking like a character involves envisioning what they might be saying. Processing dialogue as the exact words of a character will assist students in comprehending connected text. When students write dialogue, they gain a deeper understanding of the role it can play in getting to know the characters in a book.

Materials:
- talk bubbles
- chart paper
- marker

Prep Step: Prepare a sketch to match the role-play for the active engagement.

Connection

Ask, "Have you ever noticed that characters in books sometimes talk to each other? This talking between characters is called *dialogue*. Dialogue is the exact words a character is saying in the story. **Today I want to teach you how to add dialogue to your story using talk bubbles because then you can make your characters talk to each other.**"

Teach

Share a picture book that contains dialogue. The Spot series by Eric Hill is one that is simple and easy to use. Begin by inviting the class to look at the book. If you are using a Spot book it might sound like this:

"Let's look at this book about a dog named Spot. He is at the beach. Do you see those big things coming out of Spot's mouth? Those are called *talk bubbles*. You can see they each point to a character. If you read what is inside the talk bubble, you can see what the character is saying. You can do this in your writing too. Think back to a time when you were writing a story and wanted your character to say something. Maybe that character was you or your mom or a friend. A talk bubble will let your

reader know what you or your mom or your friend actually said. Eric Hill did this in his story about his dog Spot. He wanted us to know exactly what Spot said so he used a talk bubble to tell us. He made Spot talk. The talk bubble allowed the reader to hear his words."

Active Engagement

Role-play a little scenario. Have the class watch you do something and then listen for the words you say. Then invite them to turn and tell their partner the exact words they heard you say. Show the class the sketch you prepared of the scene of your role-play. Add a talk bubble and write in the exact words that you said. Share that you could also write those words in the sentence under the picture as well.

Link to Future Work

Encourage students to use a talk bubble to make their characters' words visible to the reader.

Follow Up

This lesson is a prerequisite to the next lesson on dialogue. Talk bubbles can also be used for sound words. ●

Writing with Dialogue

Reading Connection: Extending the role of dialogue to include longer sentences will provide students with a venue for re-reading their pieces with expression and feeling. This will also continue the practice of paying attention to the voices of characters in connected text.

Materials:
- Big Book with dialogue

Prep Step: Have class-shared story on a chart.

Connection

Ask students if they agree that people talk all day long. They talk to get things they want, they talk to tell others how they are feeling, they talk to give information. People like to talk. Read an excerpt from a book that uses dialogue. Remind students of the work they did with talk bubbles. Remind them that when people talk in books, it is called *dialogue*. Authors don't always use talk bubbles. They also use dialogue within their text. **Today I want to teach you how write dialogue within your stories.**

Teach

Discuss the reasons for including dialogue in a piece. Share with students that by making characters in your story talk it makes the reader feel like he is right there with you, listening in. Share a page from a Big Book that contains dialogue. Point out the quotation marks. These marks are what help the reader know that these are the exact words of the character. Explain that quotation marks go around the words. To the reader, quotation marks are just like a speech bubble hanging over the character's head. Explain that the word *said* is often a signal word that the character is about to talk.

Return to a class-shared story. Find a spot where dialogue would be appropriate. Ask students to share what was actually said during the moments written into the class story. Insert the dialogue in the appropriate place as the class observes. Re-read the story with the dialogue.

Active Engagement

Continue with the class story and ask the students to find another spot where dialogue would be appropriate. Have them turn and tell their partners their idea.

Link to Future Work

Encourage students to go back to their folders and find a previous story where dialogue could be added. Another way to practice would be to insert dialogue in a new story.

Follow Up

Don't be concerned if dialogue takes over a student piece. Often when students are introduced to something new, they overdo it. When students begin to use dialogue correctly, you will be able to teach into the use of quotation marks. This is probably most effective in individual conferences. You will find students approximating their use and that is fine. Point out where quotation marks go and coach students to place them in the appropriate place. Once you see students including dialogue successfully, they can move on to using better words than *said*. ●

CRAFT MINI-LESSON 7
Writing with a Variety of Speaker Tags

Reading Connection: Identifying what a character is feeling assists the reader in making personal connections. Students will read differently once they recognize the role of the speaker tag. Teaching students to use better words than *said* will deepen their understanding of why reading the words as the author intended enhances meaning.

Materials:
- picture book with dialogue
- chart paper
- marker
- sentence strips

Prep: Prepare sentence strips found under active engagement.

Connection

Remind students of the work they have been doing with dialogue. Remind them that the word *said* signals to the reader that someone is about to talk in the story. Explain the importance of using a more specific word than *said*. **Today I want to teach you how to use specific speaker tags to let your reader know exactly how your character sounds when they talk.**

Teach

Read a page or two from a picture book that contains dialogue with many different speaker tags (*Peter's Chair* by Ezra Jack Keats works well). After reading, have students call out the words that replaced *said*. Some examples might be *called, whispered, muttered,* and *shouted.* Record the different speaker tags. Re-read them together in the tone that the word suggests. For example, if the word is *whisper,* then whisper the word. Explain that the author wants you hear the words the way the character actually spoke them. The word *said* does not do that.

Active Engagement

Write this sentence on a sheet of chart paper, *"Today is a school day," said the class.* Invite students to read it with you. Share that the sentence sounds dull because you aren't exactly sure how to read it. Are you supposed to be excited that it is a school

day or sad that it is a school day? Then show the students the same sentence only with an identified speaker tag. You can write these on sentence strips and show them one at a time or write them on a chart and just uncover one at a time:

"Today is a school day," shouted the class.
"Today is a school day," whispered the class.
"Today is a school day," moaned the class.
"Today is a school day," screeched the class.

Ask students to read the sentences again with their partners and to make sure they are reading them as the author intended. Then ask specific students to read the sentences. Finally, have students re-read the sentences together. Emphasize the importance of using a better word than *said.*

Link to Future Work

Remind students that it is their job as authors to let their reader know how to read their piece. Share that if they are using dialogue in their piece to remember to use a more specific word than *said* because it will help their reader understand and enjoy their story.

Follow Up

Point out specific speaker tags when you read them in shared class books. You could make a class or individual charts for students to use as a reference. Reinforce the appropriate use of quotation marks with dialogue in individual conferences. ●

CRAFT MINI-LESSON 8
Showing Your Reader what Your Characters are Feeling and Thinking

Reading Connection: The ability to infer requires readers to mesh what they know about a character with their own background knowledge. Students can practice the act of sharing internal thinking through their writing. In turn, while reading, students can more easily decipher the internal thoughts of the characters found in the story.

Materials:
- *The Bear, the Mouse, and the Red Ripe Strawberry* by Audrey Wood (or any book that shows a character using internal thinking)

Prep Step: Mark the pages to read in the above picture book.

Connection

Share that writers always tell the action in their stories using words that make the reader see what is happening. But sometimes the whole story isn't only on the outside, there is the inside part of the story as well. This is the part of the story where the character is thinking or feeling something. Discuss how you can't just look at someone and know what they are thinking. The same is true in writing: you can't possibly know what is going on inside the character's head unless the author tells you. **Today I want to teach you how to include the inside and the outside part of your story so your reader will know what your characters are feeling or thinking.**

Teach

Give an example of one of your story ideas. For example, "I was walking to lunch with my friends on a beautiful sunny day. The sky was as blue as water. The birds were singing and I was carrying my new lunchbox." After sharing those sentences aloud, ask the class if they think you were happy. Then say, "It does sound like I am happy, but it would be hard for you to tell for sure unless I told you."

Share that maybe you should add your internal thinking about how you were happy because it was your turn to be the table washer and that you had always wanted to be the table washer. Think aloud about how important it would be to share that information with your reader. Re-tell your story, inserting your inside thinking. So now it would sound like: "I was walking to lunch with my friends on a beautiful sunny day. The sky was as blue as water. The birds were singing and I was carrying my new lunchbox. But that wasn't the best part. The best part was that it was my turn to wash the tables. I had been waiting all year to wash the tables. I was so excited!"

Compare the two kinds of thought. Discuss how it's almost like you are writing two stories when you share the inside thoughts of a character while telling the outside action. Remind students that both are important to the meaning.

Active Engagement

Share *The Bear, the Mouse and the Red Ripe Strawberry* by Don and Audrey Wood. This is a story about a little mouse who just picked a strawberry, the bear's very favorite food. Read a couple of pages and ask the class to listen for the outside story. Then share that they will be adding the inside story. Share these conversation stems:

How do you think this mouse is feeling?
What might he be thinking?

Ask students to turn and tell their partner the answers to these questions. Invite them to share what could be added to tell the inside story of the little mouse. Listen to ideas and choose one to write as the inside story to the book.

Link to Future Work

Challenge the class to choose a story idea that they can use to write both the outside and inside stories. Remind them that the inside story is telling the reader what the characters are thinking or feeling. The outside story is the characters' action. Invite students to add inside thinking to a former piece or to try this technique in a new piece.

Follow Up

This lesson will have to be repeated often for transfer to occur. Teaching students how to use the signal word, *thought*, might help to remind students to add internal thinking to their pieces. ●

Outside Story

Setting-Where is the story taking place?

Characters-Who is the story happening to?

Action-What is happening that your reader can picture?

Inside Story

Feelings-What is the character feeling?

Thoughts-What is your character thinking?

CRAFT MINI-LESSON 9
Writing with Details

Reading Connection: Providing details paints the visual images that allow readers to make sense of text. Details allow simple scenes to come alive with sights and sounds. Model for students how to pick details out of connected text to enhance meaning. Students will want to complete the whole picture for their reader as well. Writing with details will allow this to happen.

Material:
- three-dimensional object

Prep Step: Write the story of your three dimensional object on chart paper on the bottom of this page.

Connection

Remind students that the way we discover the world around us is through our five senses (*sight, sound, smell, taste,* and *touch*). Share that these senses provide the entry into the details of our lives. **Today I want to teach you how to write with details so your reader will see exactly what you want them to see.**

Teach

Hold up a three-dimensional object, such as a stuffed animal. Allow the students to examine it closely. Allow them to hold, touch, and smell the object. Then ask for volunteers to share the details they observed. Record these on chart paper. Code each detail as *sight, sound, smell, touch,* or *taste.* Discuss which details you would use if you were going to write a story that would include this object.

Active Engagement

Read the class the story you've written about your object. Then invite the class to ask you more questions about your object. As they uncover details, find a

place to insert them into your story. Remind them the best details paint a picture in the readers mind.

Link to Future Work

Ask students to think about details in their writing. Review the five senses by requesting that students hold up one hand, touch each finger and say one of the senses. Remind them to re-read their story to discover if they have details that include all five.

Follow Up

Have students underline the details in their stories to share with their partners. During conferring, you might have to help students realize that the best details are the ones that add to the picture in the reader's mind. If the detail is not important, then it doesn't need to be added. For example, if a child is writing about the trip to the zoo, the color of the shirt he is wearing probably is not important to the story.

Remind students that clear descriptions of people, places, and things will make their stories come alive. ●

My Special Bear

When I go to bed at night, I sleep with my stuffed bear. He is so soft and cuddly and he fits right into the crock of my arm. I can feel him tickle me as drift off to sleep. He smells like candy cane and reminds me of Christmas, the day he became mine.

Writing with Sound Words

Reading Connection: The use of sound is an effective technique for engaging readers. Sounds activate prior knowledge in a different area of memory. Sound is very active and makes the action feel current. Readers find sound words fun and engaging. Teaching students how to insert their own sound words will raise their level of writing.

Materials:
- picture book containing sound words (see bibliography on page 148 for suggestions)

Prep: Write the Teach story on a piece of chart paper.

Connection

Engage with the class a conversation about the sounds made by different objects. Some examples might include: car, truck, baby, train, basketball, etc. Share that sounds usually get our attention. Make the analogy of when someone walks into the classroom and the door squeaks. Everyone turns around and looks. Share that sounds are important in writing too, they get the reader's attention. **Today I want to teach you how to write with sound words.**

Teach

Share a few pages of a picture book that contains sound words. Some examples can be found in the bibliography. Point out the sound words and share how they make the reader feel right there in the moment with the author. Display the following story on a sheet of chart paper:

"The basketball game was exciting. The ball bounced between the players. One player tried to hit the ball out of bounds. Another player tried to catch it but fell on the floor. Then number 12 grabbed the ball and shot the basket in the hoop. The crowd cheered."

Ask for feedback about your story. Then discuss how adding sound words could make your story more realistic. Think aloud about a sound that would match the action in every sentence and then add the sound word. It might sound like this:

"Hmm, the ball bounced between the players...

what sound did that make? It made a *thump* sound. So I will add that to my sentence. Now it will read, 'The ball bounced between the players, thump, thump, thump.'"

Follow this same procedure until you have sound words added to each sentence. Re-read the piece and verify that the story is more exciting with the sound words.

Active Engagement

Give students some scenarios and have them share out the sound they would hear. Some examples might include

- a swing at the playground
- footsteps in the hall
- an owl at night
- children in the pool
- someone eating an apple
- fireworks

Link to Future Work

Remind students to always be on the lookout for sounds they could add to their stories. Challenge them to use at least two sound words in their pieces today.

Follow Up

Make a class mural and add speech bubbles with sound words. ●

Adding On to the Middle of a Piece

Reading Connection: Recognizing that most of the action in a narrative is found in the middle of the story is important for beginning readers. This realization will allow them to find the gist of the story. In a non-narrative piece, lack of important information will misinform the reader. Scrutinizing the middle for missing information will allow students to read with an interchangeable lens.

Materials:
- shared class story (with missing event) on chart paper
- sentence strip
- scissors and tape
- teacher-written story to match the chart paper across pages with the flap already added

Prep Step: Prepare flaps. Write class story on chart paper.

Connection

Declare that you have been noticing many writers going back and re-reading their stories, a really great thing. Share a personal vignette about your experience with re-reading. Share that often when you go back and re-read your piece, you realize that you have left something out, often a really important sentence. Ask for a show of thumbs up if that has happened to any of them. **Today I want to teach you how to add on something you have forgotten, even if it is in the middle of your piece.**

Teach

Write a class story on chart paper. Deliberately leave out an event. Re-read the story aloud. Discuss whether there is any information missing. After identifying the missing information, share how you can add it to the piece using a flap. On a sentence strip, write the missing information and tape it as a flap onto the chart at the point where the missing information should go. Explain that a flap will hold the information that is missing. Re-read the piece with the flap.

The flap should resemble this picture.

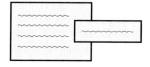

Active Engagement

Reproduce nursery rhyme at bottom of page, copy it, and give each student a copy along with one sentence strip. Have students work in pairs to write the missing sentence on the flap and tape it to the rhyme. Re-read the story together.

Link to Future Work

Remind students that they will always have a tool to add on forgotten information in their stories. Flaps can be used at any point of their story.

Follow Up

Expect to see many, many flaps once this lesson has been taught. You may have to have a lesson around appropriate use of the flap reiterating that the flap is only for important information left out. Keep flaps and tape in the writing center. Management of these materials will probably require a lesson as well. ●

Jack and Jill went up the hill
To fetch a pail of water
And Jill came tumbling after

Using Strong Verbs

Reading Connection: Students should be able to identify nouns and verbs within a sentence. Identifying these parts of speech will assist in retelling a story and monitoring for comprehension. Once students understand the job of a strong verb, they will be able to use them with intention in their own writing.

Materials:
- chart paper

Prep Step: Write the following sentence on a sheet of chart paper: My dog runs after rabbits.

Connection

Define a *noun* as *a word that stands for a person, place or thing.* Define a *verb* as *a word that describes an action.* Explain that sentences contain both of these types of words. **Today I want to teach you how to write with strong verbs that show lots of action.**

Teach

Describe a few items that are strong: a piece of metal, a steel bridge, a strongman. etc. If something is strong it can hold a lot of weight. Share that strong verbs hold a lot of weight in a sentence. Action is what keeps the reader interested, and it must be so powerful that that action feels like it is happening right in the moment. Share this example: "Today I am going to write the story of when my cat chased a squirrel across my yard. I really want to paint the picture clearly for my reader because it is so funny. I'm going to pretend like this story is happening right now in front of me. *My kitty spots a squirrel. He crouches way down low and wiggles his tail. Then he leaps forward and races across the yard. The poor squirrel scampers up a tree.* Did you hear the action? My kitty *spots, crouches, wiggles, leaps,* and *races.* Those are strong verbs that paint a picture when

you close your eyes. These are very specific or exact words. *Races* mean something more specific than *runs. Leaps* is more specific than *jump. Race* and *leap* are strong verbs. If I just wrote, 'My kitty runs after squirrels,' it just wouldn't have painted the same picture."

Active Engagement

Write the following sentence on chart paper: *My dog runs after rabbits.* Have students work with a partner to think of stronger verbs to share the action. Remind them to think of an action word that is very specific and would explain exactly what a dog might do as he chases a rabbit. Listen in and share out their ideas. Retell the action back to the class using some of the stronger verbs.

Link to Future Work

Encourage students to think hard about the action in each sentence and choose a word that is specific and strong.

Follow Up

Invite students to be strong verb detectives as they read. Make charts of strong verbs to be used as a resource for students as they write. ●

Using Patterns to Create a Mood

Reading Connection: Text structure is one way to support beginning readers and writers. Showing students the way text is put together will assist them in discovering pieces of text that are predictable and familiar. Learning how the text works during writing will help students recognize the same structure as they read.

Materials:
- chart paper

Prep Step: None.

Connection

Identify a few familiar structures from class read alouds. Some examples might be a *repeating line*, *question/answer*, *organized in a list*, etc. Remind students of how the structure (the way a text is organized) is an important way that an author can force is reader to focus on what is important. **Today I want to teach you how to use a pattern to create a mood in your piece.**

Teach

Identify several different moods. For example, *spooky, happy, grumpy*, etc. Write these on a chart. Share how you can use the structure of a repeating line to create one of those moods. It might sound like this. "Today I am going to write a spooky story about the time I went into the attic all by myself. I want to create a mood in my piece so that my reader knows this is a spooky story. I am going to use the same words over and over to make my piece sound scary. This is called a *repeating line*. Let me think of some scary words I could use to start each page. *Spooky, scary, dark, screechy, smelly*— those are all words I could use. I could write, 'In the spooky, screechy, attic I poked around. In the spooky, screechy attic, I found a familiar box. In the spooky, screechy attic, I opened the box carefully. In the spooky, screechy, attic I couldn't believe my eyes.'

"Did you hear how I did that? I thought of the mood I wanted to create. Then I thought of some words that would create that mood. Finally, I put those words together to make a repeating line to start each new page."

Active Engagement

With a partner, have students choose a mood from the chart. Have them work together to choose some words that would portray that mood. Then ask them to put those words together to make a repeating line. Invite students to share their mood and their repeating line.

Link to Future Work

Encourage students to try to use a repeating line as one way to create a mood in their piece. Have students who do this work successfully share their lines with the class.

Follow Up

Create a tub of books that contain a repeating line for the classroom library. Some examples can be found in the bibliography on page 149. Have students place a sticky note in their own independent reading books when they find a repeating line. Ask them to think about the mood created by the repeating line. ●

Studying an Author You Love

Reading Connection: Reading like a writer is the essence of reading well. When students are encouraged to study the writing of a particular author they will discover the intent of specific writing techniques and strive to try them out in their own writing.

Materials:
- several books by the mentor author
- study chart

Prep Step: Create an author study chart.

Connection

Using an author as a mentor in writing serves two purposes. First, students become acquainted deeply with an author through the study of his writing. In turn, students can envision the same techniques in their own writing. Taking advantage of the expertise of the multitude of published authors will bring many benefits to a classroom.

Find an author who you and your children love and who writes in a style that your children will understand. A few who young children enjoy include Ezra Jack Keats, Angela Johnson, Donald Crews, Mercer Mayer, and Eric Carle. After choosing one author, immerse your students in read alouds of their books. Provide a browsing basket and allow students to read these books over and over. One day, begin writer's workshop by saying **Today I want to teach you how to study the work of _____ because she is an author just like you and she has some writing techniques to teach us.**

Teach

Before you begin the study, review the books of your chosen author and choose a few techniques he or she uses to teach to the class. For example, Ezra Jack Keats uses ellipses, hyphens, and strong settings in almost all of his books. Angela Johnson uses small moments and sound words. The techniques

that bubble to the top are the one you will want to teach your students to emulate. Make a chart the resembles the one on page 145. As you teach a technique to the class, add it to the chart. Then encourage the class to try it out in their own writing.

Active Engagement

Throughout the author study, provide time for students to read the books of your chosen author and notice independently what they see the author doing. Discuss their observations and add them to the class chart as well.

Link to Future Work

Continue to study the work of your mentor author in reading and writing. Encourage students to find other authors who write with the same techniques.

Follow Up

An author study should take about three weeks. During this time, immerse students in the work of the mentor author through read alouds, partnership work, independent reading, and independent writing. Allow time to discuss student discoveries and envision those discoveries in student work. Celebrate the end of the study be sharing student work written under the influence of the mentor author. ●

An Author We Love: _____

What writing technique did we notice?	What do we call this technique?	What does this technique do in a piece of writing?	Name of the book where we found it.

— CHAPTER NINE —
Final Thoughts

Many educators feel that the National Reading Panel deliberately snubbed the teaching of writing in their 2000 report. They identified five essential components necessary for teaching reading (phonemic awareness, phonics, vocabulary, fluency, and comprehension), but oral language and writing were not highlighted in the report.

The National Reading Panel never suggested that writing should not be practiced. Process writing was just not included as a component of the 90-minute reading block required for implementation of the Reading First Grant. Teachers in Reading First schools began to scramble to find time in the day to teach writing. This has always been a mystery to me. Reading First only mandates 90 minutes for the teaching of reading. I am sure all teachers of young readers and writers spend much more time than 90 minutes engaged in the teaching of literacy.

The reality remains that we need to teach smarter within the face time that we have with our students. When we think about the National Reading Panel's five components for teaching reading, we see that those same components also support oral language and writing. We must teach oral language, reading, and writing simultaneously throughout the day. Each of these areas of literacy is essential. Teachers must use their understanding of how the three are connected in order to implement thoughtful, planned instruction. This instruction must be deliberate and with purpose. It is our job to weave this thread throughout the day.

We want to teach students to be flexible with their literacy. We must frequently remind them that the purpose for both reading and writing is the making of meaning. If the words on a page mean nothing, whether the student wrote them himself or if someone else wrote them, a whole new world is lost.

Donald Graves said in a speech in Tampa, Florida, that it is easier to put something back together once you have taken it apart. Katie Wood Ray uses the analogy of a magician's sleight-of-hand: anyone who wants to learn how to perform it will need to watch it again and again to figure out how it is done. We need to understand that when our students are watching how the writing trick is done, they are also building an understanding of how the reading trick is done.

We need to continue to reflect on our teaching in both reading and writing. Use the following guiding questions to get you started:

How can I connect the conversations in both the reading and writing workshop?
What can I learn about the readers in my classroom through their writing?
What can my students learn about reading through writing?
How can I use writing to think about and respond to reading?

Literature that Supports a Writing/ Reading Connection

List and Label Books

Berkes, Marianne. 2004. *Over in the Ocean In a Coral Reef.* New York, NY. Scholastic.

Crews, Donald. 1978. *Freight Train.* New York, NY: Scholastic.

Crews, Donald.1980. *Trucks.* New York, NY: Greenwillow.

Fox, Mem. 1996. *Zoo Looking.* New York, NY. Mondo

Got, Yves. 2000. *Sam's Big Book of Words.* San Franciso, CA: Chronicle Books LLC.

Konigsburg, E.L. 1990. *Samuel Todd's Book of Great Colors.* New York, NY. Simon & Shuster

Parr, Todd. 2001. *Reading Makes You Feel Good.* New York, NY: Little Brown.

Spanyol, Jessica. 2001. *Carlo Likes Reading.* Cambridge, MA: Candlewick Press.

Riddles

Brown, Margaret Wise. 1949. *The Important Book.* New York, NY. Harper & Row.

Cohlene, Terri. 2005. *Something Special.* Bellevue, WA. Illumination Arts.

Serfozo, Mary. 1996. *What's What? A Guessing Game.* New York, NY. Simon & Shuster.

Small Moments of Time

Aragon, Jane Chelsea. 1989. *Salt Hands.* New York, NY: Penguin Press.

Brinkloe, Julie. 1995. *Fireflies.* New York, NY: Simon & Shuster.

Freeze, Marla. 2003. *Roller Coaster.* New York: NY: Harcourt.

Johnson, Angela. 1994. *Night Whispers.* New York, NY: Orchard Press.

Johnson, Angela. 1996. *The Leaving Morning.* New York, NY: Orchard Press.

Keats, Ezra Jack. 1962.*The Snowy Day.* New York, NY: Penguin Press.

Penn, Audrey. 1993. *The Kissing Hand.* New York, NY: Scholastic.

Williams, Vera B. 1982. *A Chair For My Mother.* New York: NY: Scholastic.

Yolen, Jane. 1987. *Owl Moon.* New York: NY: Scholastic.

Zolotow, Charlotte. 1993. *The Moon Was the Best.* New York, NY: Greenwillow Books.

Show, Not Tell

Allard, Henry. 1997. *Miss Nelson is Missing.* New York, NY: Houghton Mifflin.

Banks, Kate. 1995. *The Great Blue House.* New York, NY: Frances Foster Publishing.

Crews, Donald. 1998. *Night at the Fair.* New York, NY: Greenwillow.

Lovell, Patty. 2001. *Stand Tall, Molly Lou Melon.* New York, NY: G.P. Putnam Son's.

Lessac, Frane. 1995. *My Little Island.* New York, NY: Harper Collins.

Ryan, Munoz Pam. 2001. *Hello Ocean.* Watertown, MA: Charlesbridge Publishing.

Rylant, Cynthia. 1995. *The Relatives Came.* New York, NY: Simon and Schuster.

Viorst, Judith. 1972. *Alexander and the Terrible, Horrible, No Good, Very Bad Day.* New York, NY: Aladdin.

Conversation and Speech Bubbles

Brady, Margaret Park. 2001. *Now What Can I Do?* New York, NY: Sea Star.

Cameron, Polly. 1961. *"I Can't," Said the Ant."* New York, NY: Scholastic.

Chrislelow, Eileen. 1995. *What Do Author's Do?* New York, NY: Houghton Mifflin.

Hill, Eric. 1985. *Spot Goes to the Beach.* New York, NY: Putman.

McNaughton, Colin. 1999. *Shh! (Don't Tell Mr. Wolf!)* Orlando, Fl: Harcourt.

Williams, Vera B. 1990. *"More! More! More!" Said the Baby.* New York, NY: Greenwillow Books.

Different Types of Leads

Crews, Donald. 1991. *Bigmama's.* New York, NY: Greenwillow Books.

Galdone, Paul. 1973. *The Little Red Hen.* New York, NY: Houghton Mifflin.

Rylant, Cynthia. 1985. *The Relatives Came.* New York, NY: Simon & Schuster.

Siebert, Diane. 1988. *Mojave.* New York, NY: Harper Collins.

Stevens, Janet. 1990. *Cook-a-Doodle-Do.* Orlando, Fl: Harcourt Brace.

How-To Books

Brown, Lisa. 2006. *How to Be.* New York, NY: Harper Collins.

Gibbons, Gail. 1992. *Sharks.* New York, NY: Scholastic.

Gibbons, Gail. 1993. *Spiders.* New York: NY: Scholastic.

Gibbons, Gail. 1998. *The Pumpkin Book.* New York, NY: Scholastic.

Sound Words

Andrews, Sylvia. 1995. *Rattlebone Rock.* New York, NY: Harper Trophy.

Fox, Mem. 1989. *Night Noises.* New York: NY: Harcourt Brace.

Similes

Piven, Hanoch. 2007. *My Dog is as Smelly as Dirty Socks and Other Family Portraits.* New York, NY: Random House.

Wood, Audrey. 1996. *Quick as a Cricket.* Boston, MA: Houghton Mifflin.

Zahres, Wade. 2001. *Big, Bad and a Little Bit Scary.* New York, NY: Scholastic.

Strong Verbs

Ryder, Joanne. 1994. *My Father's Hands.* New York: NY: William Morrow and Company.

Zolotow, Charlotte. 1952. *The Storm Book.* New York: NY: Harper Collins.

Strong Adjectives

Brown, Ruth. 1996. *Toad.* New York, NY: Scholastic.

Heiligman, Deborah. 2005. *Fun Dog, Sun Dog.* Tarrytown, NY: Marshall Cavendish.

Voirst, Judith. 1972. *Alexander and the Terrible, Horrible, No Good, Very Bad Day.* New York, NY: Scholastic.

Picture Books Written With Patterns

Brown, Margaret Wise. 1949. *The Important Book.* New York, NY: Trophy Publishing.

Bouchard, David. 1995. *If You're Not From the Prairie.* New York, NY: Aladdin.

Johnson, Angela. 1990. *Do Like Kyla.* New York, NY: Scholastic.

Johnson, Steve and Page, Robin. 2003. *What Do You Do With a Tail Like This?* New York, NY: Houghton Mifflin.

Numeroff, Laura. 2003. *If You Give a Pig a Party.* New York, NY: Harper Collins.

Picture Books Written in Letter Format

Ahlberg, Janet and Allan. 1991. *The Jolly Postman.* New York, NY: Scholastic.

Asch, Frank. 1999. *Dear Brother.* New York, NY: Simon & Schuster.

James, Simon. 1991. *Dear Mr. Blueberry.* New York, NY: Aladdin.

Williams, Vera B. and Williams, Jennifer. 2001. *Stringbean's Trip to the Shining Sea:* York, NY: Mulberry.

Bibliography of Professional Resources

Adams, M.J. (1990). *Beginning to read: Thinking and learning about print.* Cambridge, MA: MIT Press.

Anderson-McElveen, S., & Dierking, C. (1999) *Teaching writing with children's literature.* Gainesville, FL: Maupin House.

Beck, I., McKeown, & M., Kucan, L. (2002) *Bringing words to life.* New York, NY: The Guildford Press.

Block, C.C., & Israel, S.E., (2005) *Reading first and beyond.* Thousand Oaks, CA: Corwin Press.

Booth, D. & Roswell, J. (2002). *The literacy principal: leading, supporting and assessing reading and writing initiatives.* Toronto: Canada: Pembroke Publishers.

Brand, M. (2004). *Word savy: Integrated vocabulary, spelling, & word study,* Portland, ME: Stenhouse.

Calkins, L.M. (1994). *The art of teaching writing.* Portmouth, NH: Heinemann.

Calkins, L.M. (1994). *The art of teaching reading.* Portsmouth, NH: Heinemann.

Calkins, L.M., & Hartman, A., & White, Z. (2005). *One to one: The art of conferring with young writers.* New York: NY: Heinemann.

Cambourne, B. (1998). *The whole story.* New York: Ashton Scholastic.

Clay, M.M. (2002). *An observational survey of early literacy achievement* (2nd ed.). Portsmouth, N.H.: Heinemann.

Cooper, J.D. (1999) *Literacy: Helping children construct meaning.* (4th ed) New York: NY: Houghton Mifflin.

Dierking, C., & Jones, S. (2003) *Growing up writing: Mini-lessons for emergent and beginning writers.* Gainesville, FL: Maupin House.

Dorn, L.J., French, C., Jones, T., (1998). *Apprenticeship in literacy: Transitions across reading and writing.* Portland, ME: Stenhouse.

Ellery, V.,(2005). *Creating strategic readers: tenigues for developing competency in phonemic awareness, phonics, fluency, vocabulary, and comprehension.* Newark, DE: International Reading Association.

Ehri, L., & Snowling, M.J., *Developmental Variation in Word Recognition. Journal of Research in Reading*, 18, 116-125

Fletcher, R., & Portalupi, J.(2001). *Writing workshop: The essential guide.* Portsmouth, NH: Heinemann.

Fountas, I.C. & Pinnell, G.S. (1996). *Guided reading: Good first teaching for all children.* Portsmouth, NH: Heinemann.

Fountas, I.C. & Pinnell, G.S. (1999). *Matching books to readers: Using leveled books in guided reading, K-3.* Portsmouth, NH: Heinemann.

Freeman, Marcia. *Non-fiction writing strategies: Using Science Big Books as Models.* Gainesville, FL: Maupin House.

Graves, D.H. (1982). *Writing; Teachers and children at work.* Portsmouth, NH: Heinemann.

Gentry, J.R., & Gillet, J.W. (1992) *Teaching kids to spell.* Portsmouth, NH: Heinemann.

Hansen, J. (1997) *When writers read.* Portsmouth, NH: Heinemann.

Juel, C.(1998). *Learning to read and write: A longitudinal study of fifty-four children from first through fourth grades.* Journal of Eudcational Psychology, 80, 437-447.

Keene, E., & Zimmerman, S. (1997). *Mosiac of thought: Teaching comprehension in a reader's workshop.* Portsmouth, NH: Heinemann.

Kendall, J., & Khuon Outey (2006). *Writing Sense: integrating reading and writing lessons for English language learners.* Portland, ME: Stenhouse.

Lyons, A., & Moore, P. (2003) *Sound sytems: explicit, systematic phonics in early literacy contexts.* Portland, ME: Stenhouse.

McCarrier, A., Pinnell, G.S., & Fountas, I. (1999). *Interactive writing: How language and literacy come together.* Portsmouth, NH: Heinemann.

McElveen, S. & Dierking, C. (2001). *Literature models to teach expository writing.* Gainesville, FL: Maupin House.

Mermelstein, L.,(2006) *Reading/writing connections in the K-2 classroom: find the clarity and then blur the lines.* Boston, MA: Pearson Education Inc.

Miller, D. (2002). *Reading with meaning: Teaching comprehension in the primary grades.* York: ME: Stenhouse.

Pinnell, G.S., & Fountas, I.C. (1998). *Word matters: Teaching phonics and spelling in the reading/writing classroom.* Portsmouth, NH: Heinemann.

Ray, Katie Wood with Cleaveland, Lisa B. (2004) *About the authors: Writing workshop with our youngest writers.* Portsmouth, NH: Heinemann.

Ray, Katie Wood. (2002) *What you know by heart. how to develop curriculum for your writing workshop.* Portsmouth, NH: Heinemann.

Shefelbine, J.,Litman, C. & Wilson, M. *Reading, writing, talking, thinking, and caring in the kindergarten classroom.* Kindergarten Education: Theroy, Research, and Practice Vol. 5, No.1, Spring, 2000-pp. 43-71.

Walpole, Sharon. (2007) *Phonics, word recognition, and spelling.* Georgia Reading First. http://curry.edschool.virginia.edu/reading/projects/garf/